D0185902

RELIGION

Buddha head

*The soul is like a charioteer
with two horses, one fine
and good and noble,
and the other the opposite*

PLATO IN *PHAEDRUS* (ADAPTED)

The Greek
deities Eros,
Aphrodite, and Pan

Gemstone inscribed
with verse from
the Qur'an

*The mind is wavering and restless…
let the wise straighten their minds
as makers of arrows make their
arrows straight*

GAUTAMA THE BUDDHA (ADAPTED)

*To God belongs the kingdom of the
heavens and of the earth; and God
is powerful over everything*

QUR'AN IV

Egyptian Ankh

*I am all that has ever been,
I am all that is,
I am all that ever shall be,
yet never have mortal eyes
perceived me as I am*

SONG TO THE EGYPTIAN MOTHER GODDESS NEIT

Christian plaque
showing Christ
on the cross

*I have been born again and again,
from time to time… To protect
the righteous, to destroy the wicked,
and to establish the kingdom of God,
I am reborn from age to age*

KRISHNA IN THE *BHAGAVAD GITA* IV

*Jesus Christ is the
same yesterday and
today and for ever*

HEBREWS 13: 8

Statue of Hindu
avatar Krishna

DK EYEWITNESS GUIDES

RELIGION

Written by
MYRTLE LANGLEY

A Jewish
Torah scroll

God said to Moses, "I AM WHO I AM.
This is what you are to say to the Israelites:
'I AM has sent me to you'"

EXODUS 3: 14

Dorling Kindersley

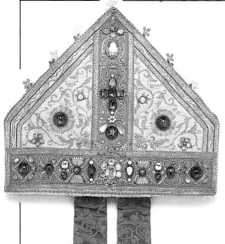

Bishop's mitre

Dorling Kindersley

**LONDON, NEW YORK, DELHI, JOHANNESBURG,
MUNICH, PARIS, and SYDNEY**

For a full catalogue, visit

DK www.dk.com

Project editor David Pickering
Art editor Sharon Spencer
Managing editor Gillian Denton
Managing art editor Julia Harris
Production Charlotte Trail
Picture research Kathy Lockley
Researcher Julie Ferris
Special photography Ellen Howden,
Andy Crawford, Geoff Dann,
Ray Moller, and Gary Ombler

This Eyewitness ® Guide has been conceived by
Dorling Kindersley Limited and Editions Gallimard

First published in Great Britain in 1996
by Dorling Kindersley Limited,
9 Henrietta Street, London WC2E 8PS

6 8 10 9 7 5

ISBN 0 7513 6075 9

Colour reproduction by Colourscan, Singapore
Printed in China by Toppan Printing Co. (Shenzhen) Ltd.

Tile with writing from the Qur'an

Christian rosary
used in prayer

Islamic tile

Hindu goddess Durga

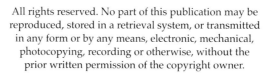

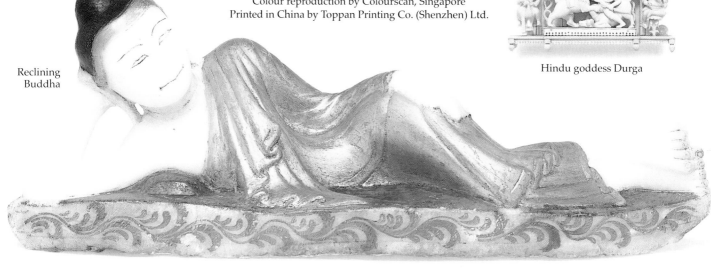

Reclining
Buddha

Jewish Seder plate
for Passover

Tibetan
prayer
wheel

Contents

Introduction

When, as tiny babies, we first enter this world, we have no experience, we know no words; our minds are not filled with thoughts and ideas. We simply exist, aware only of our immediate surroundings and secure in the love of our parents. As we grow older we become aware of ourselves and of our wider surroundings; we learn to communicate through speech as well as with the other senses. Our minds and spirits are opened up to thoughts and ideas, experience, and reflection. Questions are asked. Answers are sought. Who am I? Why is the world as it is? Why do people die? Why isn't everybody happy? What is God like? Does God really exist? The world's religions and their founders have asked these questions and given their own very different and yet at the same time very similar answers. "Know yourself." "Know God." These two precepts sum up the religious search and at the same time help us to find again the peace and happiness we knew as children.

The religious quest

THE WORLD CAN BE an uncomfortable place to live in as well as a cause for excitement and wonder. Life itself can be both puzzling and exhilarating. A person may feel very much alone although surrounded by others. To a very great extent existence and the universe remain a mystery. So, from the earliest times humankind has set out on a religious quest or spiritual search, so that life and death may take on some meaning and significance. Out of this search the world's religions have emerged. Broadly speaking, there are two main traditions. One accepts the essential goodness of the physical world but tries to change the parts of it that are wrong or broken. The other says that reality is essentially spiritual, and seeks to release the soul from an endless round of birth, death, and rebirth in the material world. Religions have several different dimensions. They teach people how to live, and tell myths – stories about the gods and creation which help to explain life. They offer their followers systems of ideas and beliefs, rituals (set patterns) of worship, social organizations to belong to, and the possibility of the experience of a greater reality.

LIGHT OF LIFE
Since ancient times, people have recognized that life on Earth depends on the Sun. So they have visualized God as light and life, and used the Sun as a symbol for God.

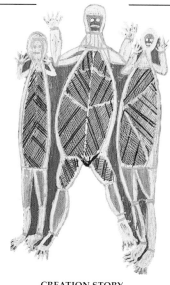

CREATION STORY
This Australian bark painting shows an Aboriginal ancestral group from the Dreamtime, a time when the landscape received its present form. In many religions, moral laws are rooted in beliefs about the creation, or beliefs about the ancestors.

Religion is not alien to us...
It is always within us:
with some consciously;
with others, unconsciously.
But it is always there

MAHATMA GANDHI

Uluru (previously known as Ayers Rock)

REACHING UPWARDS
The seven terraces of the great Buddhist monument of Borobudur in Indonesia are lined with scenes of the Buddha's spiritual progress, carved in stone. As pilgrims walk around and upwards, they learn about how to follow his example. At the top is an empty, bell-shaped dome, perhaps inviting the presence of the Buddha and his wisdom. Many religions use architecture, sculpture, and the other arts to convey their ideas.

LIFE AND DEATH

Death comes to everyone. It is both welcomed and feared. Yet many people see indications that death is not the end and this life is not the only one. In dreams, people may look at themselves from outside their own bodies. On visiting new places they feel sure that they have been there before. They imagine another life where wrongs will be righted. Some believe that the soul is endlessly reborn in different bodies, others that soul and body are reunited after death. Tombs and funeral rituals may be seen as part of the preparation for the next life.

CLEANSING AND HEALING

Water is essential to life, so springs and rivers have long featured in religion as symbols of spiritual life and centres of pilgrimage. Here, in the River Ganges, India, people drink of the holy water or bathe in it for healing and cleansing.

Islamic tombstone

The rock is 348 m (1,143 ft) high, 6 km (4 miles) long, and 2 km (1.5 miles) wide

You have made us for Yourself, and our hearts are restless until they rest in You

AUGUSTINE OF HIPPO

HOLY MOUNTAIN

The vast stone outcrop called Uluru, in Australia, is of great spiritual significance to its Aboriginal custodians. Close relationships with the earth and nature are at the heart of all Aboriginal beliefs and customs. The landscape itself is seen as full of spiritual meaning. Several other religions include similar beliefs, and a number of mountains around the world are considered holy. Some are seen as places where gods live.

The Willendorf Venus, an Earth Goddess figure

There are many sacred caves in the lower parts of the rock

FERTILITY AND THE MOTHER GODDESS

Life depends on the fertility of the earth, together with light and water from heaven. Sun God and Earth Goddess have often been pictured as coming together to produce life. Lesser gods like Thunder and Rain, and human workers make sure the land is fertile. It is likely that worship of the "Mother Goddess" – associated with springtime and harvest, sowing and reaping, and the bearing of children – is an early, if not the earliest, religious rite.

Life and death in Egypt

THE ANCIENT EGYPTIANS had many gods. The chief of them all was the sun god, who was worshipped in many different forms, and seen as responsible for all creation. The other gods each had charge of a different area of life. Believing that all events were controlled by the gods, Egyptians made many offerings to try to keep them happy, hoping that the gods would bless them. They tried to lead good lives so as to be ready for the judgement of the god Osiris, who ruled the heavenly kingdom in which Egyptians wished to live after death. They pictured this kingdom as a perfect version of Egypt, called "The Field of Reeds". To get there, the dead had to make a difficult journey through the underworld, which was called Duat. If they managed to pass Duat's monsters and lakes of fire, they faced judgement by Osiris in the Hall of Two Truths.

SIGN OF LIFE
Only gods, kings, and queens were allowed to carry the ankh, the sign of life. It showed that they had the power to give life, or take it away.

EYE OF HORUS
Wadjet eye amulets were placed on mummies to protect them. A wadjet eye represented the eye the sky god Horus lost fighting the evil Seth, god of chaos and disorder, for the throne of Egypt. Magically restored, it acquired healing properties, and symbolized the victory of good over evil. It was said to protect anything behind it.

Outer coffin of Pasenhor, one of many Libyans who settled in Egypt

Symbols were painted on mummy cases to help on the voyage to the afterlife

A HOME FOR THE SPIRIT
The Egyptians prepared for the afterlife in several ways. They mummified the bodies of the dead to make them last forever, so that a dead person's spirit would always have a home. They also filled their tombs with magical protection to help them to survive the dangerous journey across Duat, and with food and equipment they might need.

THE PLACE OF JUDGEMENT
If the dead managed to cross Duat, they had to pass a final test, set in the Hall of Two Truths. The dead person's heart was weighed in the balance against the Feather of Truth, symbol of Ma'at, goddess of order, truth, and justice, to see if it was heavy with sin. In this picture, the person passes the test and is presented to Osiris. Had he failed, the monster Ammit would have eaten his heart.

The dead person is led by the jackal-headed god Anubis

The god Thoth records the result

Ammit, devourer of the dead

The Feather of Truth

The dead person's heart is in one scale

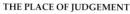

REBIRTH

Many religions have a belief in rebirth, also called new birth or second birth. This can mean passing from childhood to adulthood, awakening to spiritual life, or moving from death to life. It is often symbolized by passing through water or, as in Egypt, by leaving the grave and meeting the god of rebirth.

MAGIC SPELLS
The *Book of the Dead* is a scroll (roll) of papyrus containing a collection of magic spells. Each spell was a prayer or a plea from the dead person meant to help on the voyage through Duat to the heavenly afterlife. This statue of Osiris has a hidden compartment where the scroll was kept.

Shabti figures

Roll of papyrus

Secret compartment

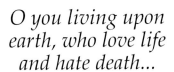

O you living upon earth, who love life and hate death...

GOD OF REBIRTH
Osiris, god of rebirth, judged people's souls in the afterlife. He was said to have triumphed over death, and every Egyptian wanted to follow his example. This statue of him would have been placed in a tomb or a temple.

Box containing the shabti figures shows gods and a priestess

Osiris presides over judgement

The guardian goddesses, Isis wife of Osiris and Nephthys her sister

WORKER FIGURES
The Egyptians believed that after death Osiris might order them to work in the fields in his heavenly land. So rich people provided their mummies with shabtis, carved figures who would spring to life and do their work for them in the afterlife.

The four Sons of Horus, guardians of the vital organs, standing on a lotus flower

Gods and nature in Greece

THE PARTHENON
Built in the 5th century BCE, the temple called the Parthenon stood on the highest point of the Acropolis in Athens. It was dedicated to the goddess Athena and housed a huge gold and ivory statue of her.

IN ANCIENT GREECE, nature was seen to hold the power of life and was therefore sacred. A mountain was the sky god's throne; the god's worshippers climbed it to pray for rain, not to admire the view. Every tree had its own spirit; the oak was sacred to Zeus, the olive to Athena, the laurel to Apollo, and the myrtle to Aphrodite. Groves were considered especially holy and were used as places of refuge. Each spring also had its nymph, each river its god, and the sea was home to many deities and spirits. Every area of life was overseen by a deity. People could choose the god they thought would help them best. The gods intervened in human life as and when they chose, helping those they liked, and harming others.

HUNTER AND MOTHER
Artemis was goddess of hunting and the moon. At Ephesus her worship merged with that of the Great Mother, an ancient goddess linked with the earth and fertility.

Eros, Aphrodite's son, also a god of love

Aphrodite appears as a graceful young woman

Pan, a wild nature god, has goat's legs and ears

The goose is a symbol of Aphrodite

APOLLO
Apollo, brother of Artemis, was the model of youthful strength and beauty. A powerful god, he was associated with the sun, light, prophecy, and healing, but if he was angry his arrows could cause plague.

GODDESS OF LOVE
Aphrodite was the goddess of love and beauty. She was also called the "foamborn" because she was said to have risen from the sea when it was sprinkled with the seed and blood of ancient, defeated gods. On this mirror case she is playing the ancient game of knucklebones with the wild, goat-like nature god Pan.

EARTH MOTHER
Demeter was goddess of the harvest. It was said that when her daughter Persephone was stolen by Pluto, king of Hades (the underworld), her sorrow made the crops stop growing. Persephone was released, on condition that she had eaten nothing in Hades. In fact, she had eaten six pomegranate seeds, so had to stay in Hades for six months each year. This story explained why we have winter and spring.

Demeter and Persephone sit side by side in this terracotta figure, probably holding the reins of an ox-cart

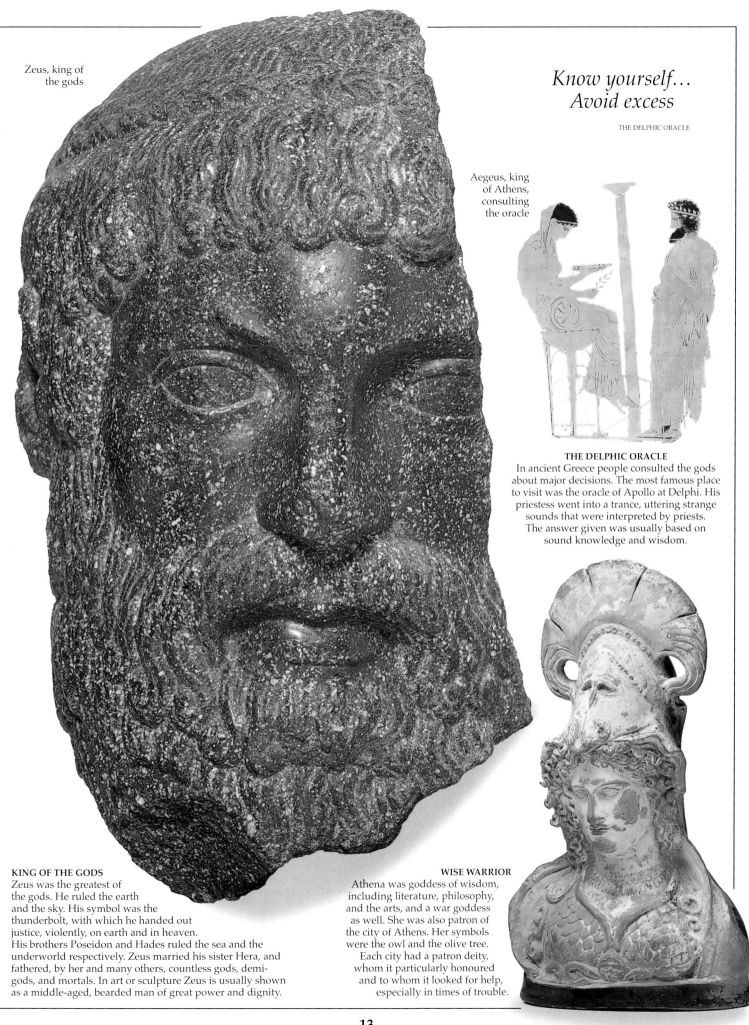

Zeus, king of
the gods

Aegeus, king
of Athens,
consulting
the oracle

THE DELPHIC ORACLE
In ancient Greece people consulted the gods
about major decisions. The most famous place
to visit was the oracle of Apollo at Delphi. His
priestess went into a trance, uttering strange
sounds that were interpreted by priests.
The answer given was usually based on
sound knowledge and wisdom.

KING OF THE GODS
Zeus was the greatest of
the gods. He ruled the earth
and the sky. His symbol was the
thunderbolt, with which he handed out
justice, violently, on earth and in heaven.
His brothers Poseidon and Hades ruled the sea and the
underworld respectively. Zeus married his sister Hera, and
fathered, by her and many others, countless gods, demi-
gods, and mortals. In art or sculpture Zeus is usually shown
as a middle-aged, bearded man of great power and dignity.

WISE WARRIOR
Athena was goddess of wisdom,
including literature, philosophy,
and the arts, and a war goddess
as well. She was also patron of
the city of Athens. Her symbols
were the owl and the olive tree.
Each city had a patron deity,
whom it particularly honoured
and to whom it looked for help,
especially in times of trouble.

The primal vision

THE POWER OF LIFE
There is a widespread belief among primal peoples that all living things are invested with mana (power). Throughout the Pacific islands of Polynesia the arts, especially wood carving, were used to represent gods, nature spirits, and the spirits of the ancestors, and to provide "vehicles" (material "homes") for their mana. This carving, from the Cook Islands, is of a god associated with canoe-making and with bringing good luck to fishermen. The same gods are found again and again among the many different peoples of Polynesia, sometimes under different names.

IN AFRICA, THE AMERICAS, and Oceania perhaps 250 million people live in "primal" or "traditional" societies. For them, all of life is religious; nothing that they think or say or do takes place outside a spiritual framework, and they look to the spiritual world for help and blessing. Those who live along Africa's Rift Valley, on the plains of the Americas, or in the Pacific, associate God with the sun and sky, and organize their lesser gods to mirror their own societies. The Maasai of East Africa worship One God linked with the sun, while the Yoruba people of Nigeria worship a High God who rules over many lesser gods. Those living in rainforests, or in densely settled areas, worship the spirits or powers of nature and venerate (give great respect and honour to) their ancestors. Rituals to do with the spirits and powers are often complex; those to do with the High God tend to be simpler.

HEALING AND HARM
In primal societies, sickness can be caused by the living or the dead. If the spirits of ancestors are not worshipped they may strike, or if the living are offended they can cast a spell. Healers use either spiritual powers or medicine to cure their patients.

African healer's charm necklace

SACRIFICE

From the earliest times, sacrifice has been offered to ancestors, spirits, or gods, to avert their anger, or express thanks, or for other reasons. It has often required the laying down of life, usually of animals such as cattle and sheep. Sometimes worshippers sacrifice by giving up pleasures or possessions.

Doll made from stick, beeswax, beads, hide

Two fertility dolls from Angola, in Southwest Africa (centre and right)

Central part of doll made from corn cob

OSHUN SHRINE
Among the Yoruba, the major goddess is Oshun, the river goddess. It is said that the work of the male gods was failing until she joined them. Women worship her if they wish to become pregnant, or to be protected from disease.

FERTILE EARTH
Many primal peoples look to the spirits and the ancestors to give them the sun, rain, and fertile earth that they need. They also need large families, and pray to spirits, ancestors, and Mother Earth to make their women fertile. In some societies girls and young women carry around fertility dolls such as these to make them fertile.

Fertility doll from Cameroon, in West Africa

The metal acts like a mirror to reflect back any evil that threatens the ancestor

Each of the three main figures carries signs of leadership: a knife, tusk, and elaborate headdress

These heads may represent family slaves

Kota guardian figure made of wood covered in brass

GUARDIAN FIGURE
Some societies believe that the physical remains of important people can hold something of the power those people had in their lifetimes. Among the Kota people of Gabon the skulls and bones of important ancestors are kept in baskets in a special hut and offerings are made to them. Guardian figures such as this are placed on such baskets to protect the ancestors' remains from evil forces.

Those who are dead are never gone

AFRICAN PROVERB

The three figures would originally have worn cloth wraps over their legs

ANCESTRAL SCREEN
It is believed that ancestors will protect and guide living relatives who honour them. Among the Kalabari people of Nigeria, screens such as this one were placed behind altars where descendants made offerings to the spirit of the ancestor depicted on the screen. On this screen, the central figure is the head of a prosperous trading house. He is standing with two sons or attendants.

Sande initiation mask

Rituals of life

Rituals of life play a major role in primal societies. They are largely of two kinds: "rites of passage" and "rites of affliction". Rites of passage take place at important moments of a person's passage through life, such as birth, puberty, marriage, divorce, and death. Rites of affliction arise at times of crisis such as illness or disaster. The rituals are usually divided into three stages: separation from the old, transition, and inclusion into the new. For example, young people at puberty may be separated from society (and, symbolically, from childhood), then instructed on how to be adults, and then incorporated back into society as full adult members of their communities. In some societies, the rituals may be performed by priests, in others by ritual leaders, or shamans, or healers.

FUNERAL DANCE
Funeral rites are important in primal religions. Among the Dogon people of West Africa they are occasions for elaborate public dances (above), accompanied by chants in a secret language. The rite retells the Dogon myth of how death entered the world – through the disobedience of young men. The Awa masked society also helps to preserve other popular Dogon myths. Here the dancers are wearing skirts dyed in red, the colour associated with death.

ELEPHANT SPIRIT MASK
Many African peoples make masks, mainly to represent the spirits when these are called on to be present at various ceremonies. Some have human features, others those of animals. They are not made to look realistic. Instead traditional, symbolic styles are followed, which are understood by ritual experts, who interpret for the people. This elephant spirit mask was made by the Igbo people of Nigeria. The elephant spirit is a symbol of ugliness.

This mask is worn on top of the head

INITIATION MASK
Among the Mende people of West Africa, young girls are initiated into the Sande society, a women's secret society, at puberty. Elders instruct them in domestic and craft skills and prepare them for marriage and motherhood. As part of the initiation a masked dance, or masquerade is held. This gives people a chance to express themselves through a ceremony which unites them. Sande masks represent power, emotion, and womanly qualities. They symbolically express the Mende ideal of female beauty.

The use of cowrie shells in decoration is widespread and usually symbolizes fertility

There is no distinction between religion and the rest of life. All of life is religious

AFRICAN SAYING

INITIATION MASK
Masks can represent important ancestors. This royal initiation mask comes from the Kuba kingdom in Zaire. It represents the son of the first divine king. Masks play an important role in initiation ceremonies. Other Kuba masks, made to look like spirits, were worn by chiefs to enforce discipline.

SPIRITS AND HEALING
In primal societies all forces which affect people, good or bad, are seen as coming from the spirits. For example, there are spirits of technology, such as the motor car, and spirits of illnesses. Sometimes these spirits, such as the Yoruba smallpox spirit above, are represented by images and are invoked (called on) for healing and blessing.

SUMMONING THE SPIRITS
Among the original peoples of the far north of North America and Asia, those who get in touch with the spirit world are known as "shamans". Shamans' masks, such as this Alaskan one, are worn at various festivals, and at rituals of healing and of divination (seeing into the future).

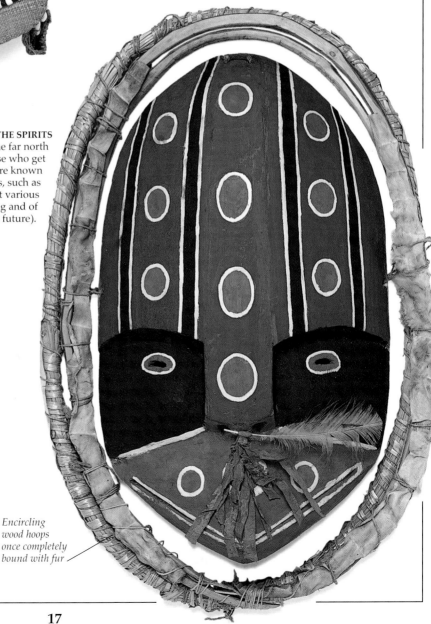

Four oval faces, each flanked by a pair of upraised hands, surround the central face of the Sun

WINTER FESTIVAL
During their winter ceremony the Bella Coola people of western Canada performed dances taught to them by the spirits of the sky. Wearing masks representing the spirits, the dancers acted out with great drama the central stories of their people's beliefs. This mask with its spherical face represents the spirit of the Sun.

Encircling wood hoops once completely bound with fur

The Hindu way

To be a Hindu is to be born a Hindu, and then to follow a certain way of life. The word "Hindu" comes from "Hind", the old Persian word for India, and Hinduism simply means the religion of the peoples of India. With no founder and no creed, it has evolved over time. As we know it today, it can be compared to a great, deep river into which, over a period of more than 3,000 years, many streams have flowed. The streams are the beliefs and practices of the numerous races, ethnic groups, and cultures of the Indian subcontinent. Hinduism has many gods, yet, for some Hindus, there is an impersonal "Absolute" behind them all, called Brahman, creator of the universe. Brahman "unfolds" into the Trimurti, the holy trinity made up of Brahma, Vishnu, and Shiva. Brahma is the creator, Vishnu the great preserver, and Shiva the destroyer but also the re-creator. Hindus everywhere believe in reincarnation, the individual soul born again in another body. Life flows on through many existences, from birth through death to rebirth. If people are good in one life, they will be rewarded by being well born in their next life.

Brahma has four heads; this sculpture shows three of them

BRAHMA THE CREATOR
Brahma's exclusive purpose is creation. Unlike Vishnu and Shiva, he does not contain opposites within himself, and so he never destroys what he has created. According to one tradition he arose out of the "egg of the universe". Originally he only had one head. He acquired three more when he created woman. After cutting her from his own body he fell in love with her, but she hid herself from him. So that he could always see her from every side, he grew heads to the right, left, and behind.

VISHNU THE PRESERVER
Vishnu contains and balances good and evil, and all other opposites, within himself. His main task, as preserver, is to maintain the divine order of the universe, keeping the balance between good and evil powers. When evil gets the upper hand Vishnu comes down to Earth to restore the balance, taking the form of one of ten incarnations called avatars – beings in whom he lives throughout their lives.

HINDUISM		
GODS?		
Brahma, Vishnu, Shiva, Sarasvati, Kali, Lakshmi, and many others		
THE AFTERLIFE?		
Reincarnation		
SCRIPTURES?		
Vedas, Upanishads, and others		
MAJOR FESTIVALS?		
Divali – New year Festival of Lights Holi – Spring festival Janmashtami – Birthday of Krishna Shivaratri – Main festival of Shiva		
SACRED ANIMAL?		
Cow is the symbol of Earth		

Smaller figures represent two of the four Vedas *(earliest holy scriptures)*

Hinduism is more a way of life than a set of beliefs

SARVEPALLI RADHAKRISHNAN, FORMER PRESIDENT OF INDIA

The flaming halo around Shiva symbolizes the cosmos

Shiva's whirling hair holds flowers, snakes, a skull, and a small figure of the goddess Ganga (the sacred river Ganges)

As Shiva beats the drum, he summons up a new creation

Shiva's vertical third eye gives light to the world

The flame is a symbol of the fire with which Shiva destroys the universe

This hand points to the left foot, beneath which the worshipper can find safe refuge

Left foot is a symbol of liberation

SHIVA AS "LORD OF THE DANCE"
Shiva is both destroyer and re-creator. He is depicted in many forms. As Nataraja, Lord of the Dance (the form shown here), he brings the dance or cycle of life to an end in order that a new cycle of life may begin. This statue illustrates a legend in which he subdued 10,000 heretics (non-believers) by dancing on the demon of ignorance.

Apasmarapurusa, the black dwarf, demon of ignorance

Shiva dances in a ring of flames

Shiva is adored by two sages (wise men); the one on his right has the lower body of a snake, the one on his left has tiger legs

This sage has the legs of a tiger

Flowers, symbols of purity, and rebirth, are used to decorate temples and statues

Gods and heroes

THE HINDU SCRIPTURES are full of the adventures of numerous gods and heroes. The *Vedas* tell of Agni the god of fire and sacrifice, Indra the sky-god of war, and Varuna the god of cosmic order. The two great Hindu epics, the *Ramayana* and *Mahabharata*, weave their tales around Rama and Krishna, the most popular of the ten avatars of Vishnu. Within the *Mahabharata* is the frequently translated great Indian spiritual classic, the *Bhagavad Gita*, the "Song of the Lord". This poem takes the form of a dialogue between the warrior Arjuna and Krishna, his charioteer, as together they fight the war between good and evil symbolized in the battle between the closely related families of the Pandavas and the Kauravas.

Matsya, the fish and first avatar, warned humanity of a great flood

Narasimha, the man-lion and fourth avatar, defeated demons

Kalki, the tenth avatar, is still to come

PRAYING IN THE GANGES
The river Ganges is a sacred river to Hindus, a symbol of life without end. Pilgrims from all over India come to bathe in its holy waters. The city of Varanasi on the Ganges is India's most sacred city and the desired place of death for every Hindu.

Krishna's skin is blue, the colour of the oceans and the sky

The flute is a symbol of the cowherds with whom Krishna spent his early years

KRISHNA AVATAR
Many colourful stories are woven around Krishna, eighth avatar of Vishnu. They are told in the great epic, the *Mahabharata*. Vishnu was persuaded to come down to Earth as Krishna when demons were about to overcome the gods. On hearing the news of Krishna's arrival, the demon-king Kansa planned to·kill him. But Krishna was fostered by a poor woman called Yashoda, who kept him safe. Countless tales are told of his childish pranks, youthful adventures, and later battles with the demons.

Krishna is standing on a lotus flower, a symbol of purity and fertility

In this ivory image Durga kills the buffalo demon Mahisha

In each of her ten hands she holds a special weapon; each weapon is a symbol of divine power

THE GODDESS DURGA
Durga (also known as Parvati and Kali) is one of the many forms assumed by Mahadevi Shakti, Shiva's consort. She is the warrior who fights demons, representing the lowest human passions. The worship of Durga often provides the opportunity for some of the greatest Hindu festivals.

In this picture, Rama and Sita sit together, with Rama's faithful brother Lakshmana behind them

Hanuman, the monkey god, loyal ally of Rama

RAMA AVATAR

Rama, seventh avatar of Vishnu, is the embodiment of goodness come down to Earth. He and his wife Sita are models of loving husband and faithful wife. He is respected as the virtuous god-king who overthrew the wicked demon Ravana. First, he and Sita were banished, then Ravana kidnapped Sita. But Rama defeated Ravana with the help of Hanuman, the brave monkey god, and his monkey army.

I am the beginning and the middle and the end of all that is. Of all knowledge I am the knowledge of the Soul

KRISHNA IN THE *BHAGAVAD GITA* 10:32

Ganesha's half-halo indicates his divinity

The crown shows kingly status

Noose to snare delusion

This decorated goad (pointed stick) represents self-control

The large flapping ears separate the essential from the non-essential

Ganesha writes with a piece of his broken tusk after his steel pen snapped

Modaka sweets

GANESHA

Ganesha is the first-born son of Shiva and his beautiful wife Parvati. It is told how Shiva, returning after a long absence to his heavenly dwelling, saw a stranger at his door and promptly cut off his head. Parvati appeared, only to find that the victim was their own son. Desperate to make amends Shiva cut off the head of a passing elephant and placed it on his son's shoulders. From that day onwards Ganesha has had an elephant's head. He is the god of wisdom and the remover of obstacles. In their prayers Hindus ask him to take note of their requests and convey them to Shiva.

Ganesha's great belly represents space, big enough to hold all wisdom and life

Three ways of salvation

HINDUS WISH TO ACHIEVE SALVATION, or moksha, by release from the cycle of rebirth. Lightening the load of karma – guilt acquired through wrong living – leads towards the final release. There are three basic ways of achieving salvation. The way of action involves performing correct religious observances, in the hope of being blessed by the divine for fulfilling these duties. The way of knowledge seeks to understand and experience the ultimate meaning of life through reason and meditation, as sadhus do. The way of devotion (the most popular way) seeks to be united with the divine through the worship of a particular deity. Traditionally Hindus are born into one of four castes (social classes), or are "untouchables" (outcastes – the lowest rank). Religious duties vary with caste.

HOLY MAN
A sadhu is a wandering holy man. He has no possessions apart from his robes and a few utensils.

WEDDING
Hindu families go to great expense to provide a wedding ceremony for their children. Marriages are arranged according to caste, kinship, and horoscope. The wedding ceremony contains many highly symbolic elements and the institution of marriage is highly valued.

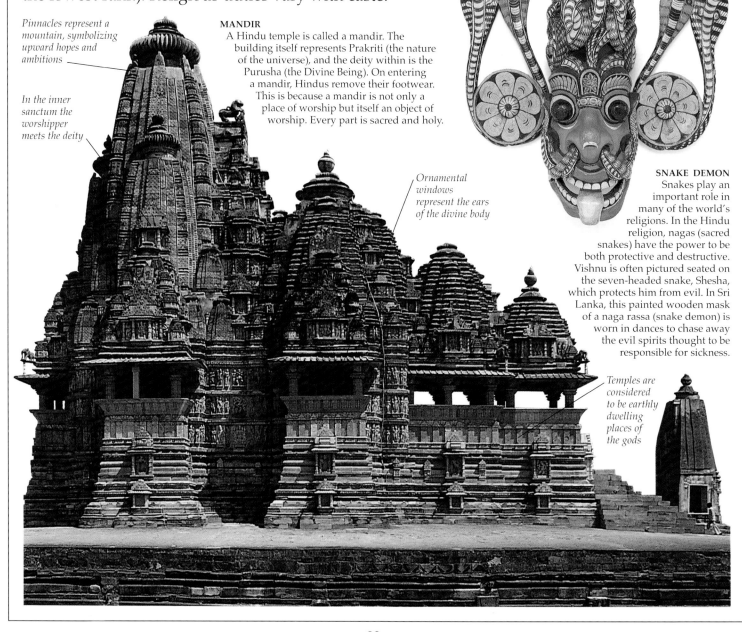

Pinnacles represent a mountain, symbolizing upward hopes and ambitions

MANDIR
A Hindu temple is called a mandir. The building itself represents Prakriti (the nature of the universe), and the deity within is the Purusha (the Divine Being). On entering a mandir, Hindus remove their footwear. This is because a mandir is not only a place of worship but itself an object of worship. Every part is sacred and holy.

In the inner sanctum the worshipper meets the deity

Ornamental windows represent the ears of the divine body

SNAKE DEMON
Snakes play an important role in many of the world's religions. In the Hindu religion, nagas (sacred snakes) have the power to be both protective and destructive. Vishnu is often pictured seated on the seven-headed snake, Shesha, which protects him from evil. In Sri Lanka, this painted wooden mask of a naga rassa (snake demon) is worn in dances to chase away the evil spirits thought to be responsible for sickness.

Temples are considered to be earthly dwelling places of the gods

INCARNATION

The idea that God or the gods make themselves known in bodily form, usually human, is found in many religions. In Hinduism, Vishnu comes down to earth a number of times in different forms known as avatars. In Christianity, God takes on human form in Jesus Christ.

Incense holder

The lotus, a symbol of purity, fertility, and creation, is linked with Vishnu

Kemal (lotus-shaped scent shaker) used in domestic worship

Main image of Vishnu

Krishna and Balarama

INCENSE
Incense is made from a number of woods and resins which, when heated or burned, give off a fragrant smell. The use of incense in divine worship is an ancient and widespread practice. It is associated with sacrifice, honour, purification, and celebration.

DAILY WORSHIP
Hindus perform puja (daily worship) not only in the temple but also in the home. Many families set aside a room for worship; others erect a shrine or image, or display a holy picture, in one corner. This is a portable shrine of Vishnu, and shows Vishnu under the protection of Shesha (the serpent), with Krishna avatar and his half-brother Balarama.

Give me your mind and give me your heart, give me your offerings and your adoration

KRISHNA IN THE *BHAGAVAD GITA 9.34*

The warrior Arjuna

Krishna, acting as Arjuna's charioteer

CHARIOT AND CHARIOTEER
In the *Bhagavad Gita* there is a dialogue between the god Krishna and the archer Arjuna on a battlefield. The battle is the war between good and evil, action and inaction, knowledge and ignorance, belief and disbelief. Krishna urges Arjuna to action and promises to be his charioteer. Vivekananda, a modern reformer and philosopher, interpreted their relationship: The body is the chariot; the outer senses are the horses; the mind the reins; and the intellect the charioteer. So man crosses the ocean of maya (illusion). He goes beyond and reaches God. When a man is under the control of his senses, he is of this world. When he has controlled the senses, he has renounced the world.

This picture shows a famous scene from the *Bhagavad Gita*

The Buddhist path

SIDDHARTHA GAUTAMA, THE FOUNDER of Buddhism, lived in the sixth century BCE in northern India. He was brought up to become a king, and married to a beautiful princess who gave him a son. As a young prince, his father protected him from all the sadness of the world outside his palaces. However, while his son was still young, Gautama managed to slip out, and encountered the "Four Sights". First was an old man, second a man sick with disease, and third a corpse being carried to the cremation ground. Finally, he saw a shaven-headed religious beggar, wearing a simple yellow robe, but radiating peace and joy. It was then that Gautama made his "Great Renunciation", leaving his family and life of great comfort to find the answers to this suffering he had seen. For six years he tried and failed, until he went to meditate under a Bodhi tree, where he received his "Great Enlightenment", and became Buddha, which means "the enlightened one".

THE NOBLE EIGHTFOLD PATH
The eight-spoked wheel is a symbol of The Eightfold Path, which is a summary of the Buddha's teaching about how to escape suffering and find enlightenment. The eight stages to follow were: right thought, right understanding, right speech, right action, right livelihood, right effort, right concentration, and right contemplation.

Eyes cast down to show he is meditating; face calm and peaceful

RENUNCIATION
Gautama's decision to leave his family is known as the Great Renunciation. For the next six years, he tried to find release from the weariness of existence. He was reduced to skin and bones, but could not reach this goal. So he left his companions and went to meditate under a Bodhi tree near the river Ganges.

Right hand points down, asking the earth to witness his enlightenment

The Buddha, meditating: in meditation Buddhists seek to empty their minds of all distracting thoughts and gain perfect peace

Buddha's cross-legged position is called the lotus position

Halo, one of the marks of Buddhahood

ENLIGHTENMENT
While meditating under the Bodhi tree, Gautama learnt "the Four Noble Truths": that all life is suffering; that the cause of suffering is desire; that the end of desire means the end of suffering; that desire can be stopped by following the Eightfold Path. The Eightfold Path is also called the Middle Way because it avoids either living for pleasure or too much self-denial.

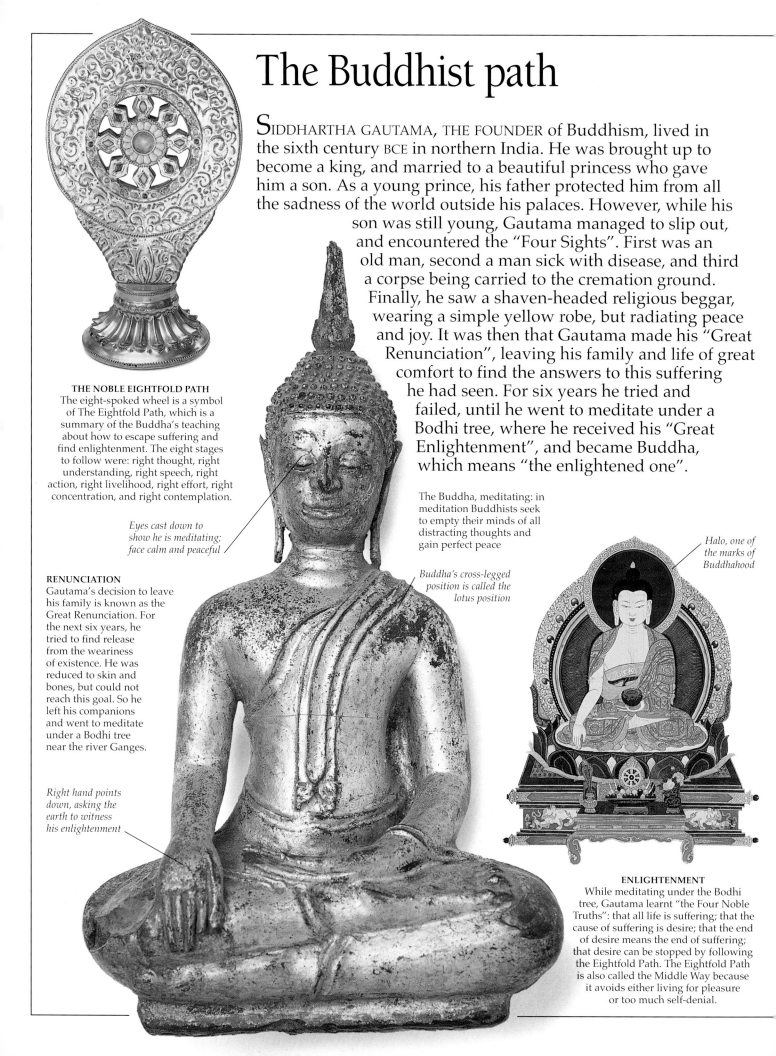

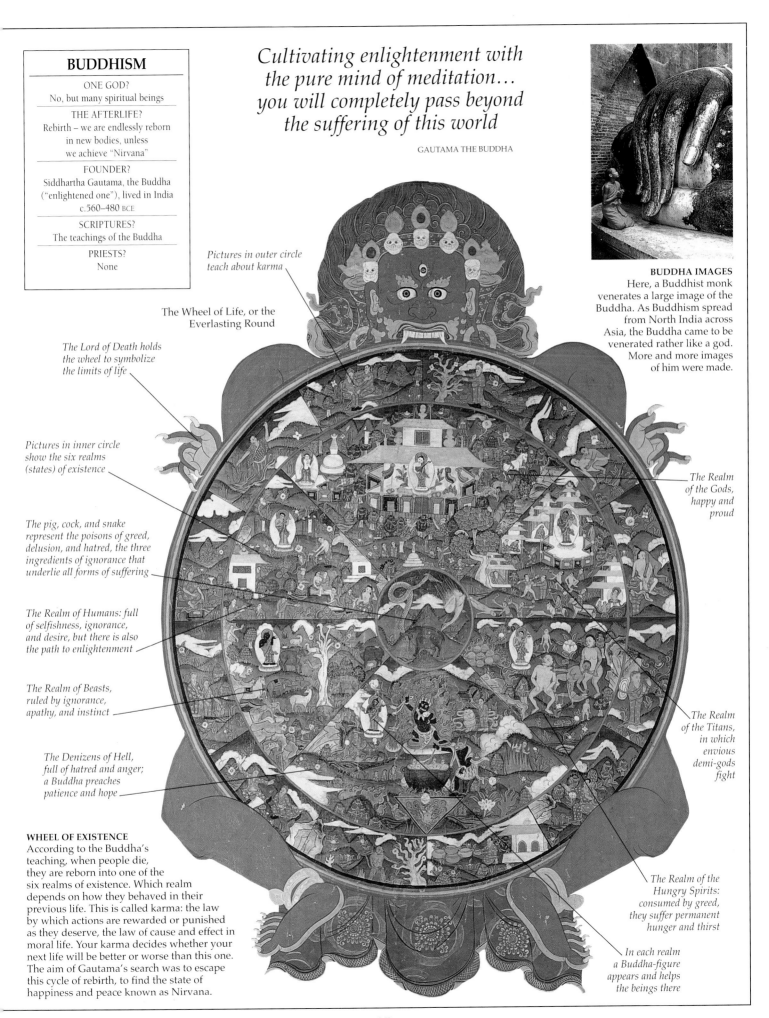

BUDDHISM

ONE GOD?
No, but many spiritual beings

THE AFTERLIFE?
Rebirth – we are endlessly reborn in new bodies, unless we achieve "Nirvana"

FOUNDER?
Siddhartha Gautama, the Buddha ("enlightened one"), lived in India c.560–480 BCE

SCRIPTURES?
The teachings of the Buddha

PRIESTS?
None

Cultivating enlightenment with the pure mind of meditation… you will completely pass beyond the suffering of this world

GAUTAMA THE BUDDHA

BUDDHA IMAGES
Here, a Buddhist monk venerates a large image of the Buddha. As Buddhism spread from North India across Asia, the Buddha came to be venerated rather like a god. More and more images of him were made.

Pictures in outer circle teach about karma

The Wheel of Life, or the Everlasting Round

The Lord of Death holds the wheel to symbolize the limits of life

Pictures in inner circle show the six realms (states) of existence

The pig, cock, and snake represent the poisons of greed, delusion, and hatred, the three ingredients of ignorance that underlie all forms of suffering

The Realm of Humans: full of selfishness, ignorance, and desire, but there is also the path to enlightenment

The Realm of Beasts, ruled by ignorance, apathy, and instinct

The Denizens of Hell, full of hatred and anger; a Buddha preaches patience and hope

The Realm of the Gods, happy and proud

The Realm of the Titans, in which envious demi-gods fight

The Realm of the Hungry Spirits: consumed by greed, they suffer permanent hunger and thirst

In each realm a Buddha-figure appears and helps the beings there

WHEEL OF EXISTENCE
According to the Buddha's teaching, when people die, they are reborn into one of the six realms of existence. Which realm depends on how they behaved in their previous life. This is called karma: the law by which actions are rewarded or punished as they deserve, the law of cause and effect in moral life. Your karma decides whether your next life will be better or worse than this one. The aim of Gautama's search was to escape this cycle of rebirth, to find the state of happiness and peace known as Nirvana.

Devotion and meditation

As BUDDHISM SPREAD OUTWARDS from India it developed into two different branches. They are often called "vehicles" since Buddhist Dharma (teaching or law) is thought of as a raft or ship carrying people across an ocean of suffering to Nirvana – a "Beyond" of salvation and bliss. Theravada, the "Little Vehicle", is mainly found in Southeast Asia. It emphasises the life of meditation lived by the monk, and its teaching tends towards the view that people are essentially on their own in the universe and can reach Nirvana only by their own efforts. Mahayana, the "Great Vehicle", is dominant in Tibet, China, Korea, Vietnam, and Japan. Mahayana Buddhists believe that people are not alone and must help one another. They can also receive help from the Buddha, and other buddhas, and from bodhisattvas (almost-buddhas who have paused before Nirvana to help others). Salvation is available to all through faith and devotion.

Monks in the precincts of the Wat Po temple in Thailand

PLACES OF WORSHIP
After the Buddha's death his body was cremated and his ashes distributed among his followers. They formed the original relics (holy objects) and were housed and worshipped in stupas (great sacred mounds). In parts of Asia stupas are called pagodas. Later, temples were built, where worship was offered in the presence of images of the Buddha and bodhisattvas.

FOCUS OF DEVOTION
Originally the Buddha was a famous and greatly honoured human being devoted to working out his own salvation and teaching others. In Mahayana Buddhism, he came to be revered as a supernatural being. His image sits in temples. Beside it there may be other buddhas, and also bodhisattvas, beings who have reached enlightenment but hold back on the threshold of Nirvana to help others find salvation.

PLACES OF MEDITATION
Buddhism gave rise to numerous sects and practices within and outside the two main vehicles. One is Zen, which originated in Chinese ways of meditation. Zen is widespread in Japan and there are Zen gardens across the country. Zen meditation has strict rules. The most important are to sit in the lotus position and to address riddles which have no answer (these help in breaking free from the mind). For example, "When you clap hands you hear a sound. Now listen to one hand clapping."

Bodhisattva Avalokiteshvara (which means "The lord who looks down")

Buddha Amoghasiddhi, one of the five "meditation buddhas"

Dipankara Buddha, the "causer of light"

Seven other bodhisattvas

Worn round hips

Worn over shoulder

Worn on top for ceremonial occasions or for travelling

Belt or girdle

Razor

Needle and thread

Sharpening stone

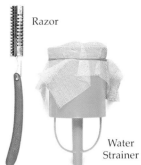

Water Strainer

To the Buddha for refuge I go
To the Dharma for refuge I go
To the Sangha for refuge I go

GAUTAMA THE BUDDHA

THAI MONK'S EQUIPMENT
Buddhist monks have very few possessions and live very simple lives. In their daily devotions, both monks and lay people (ordinary people) undertake not to cause injury, steal, consume intoxicating things, commit wrong sexual behaviour, or deceive.

Alms bowl

REINCARNATION
The belief that we live many different lives on earth. When we die we spend time in a disembodied state before being reborn in a different bodily form. What we are reborn as depends on our previous behaviour (this is the law of karma). Buddhist and Hindu forms of this belief differ. Buddhists prefer the word rebirth.

Lid from alms bowl used as plate

MONK IN MEDITATION
After his enlightenment the Buddha formed a community of monks. Ever since, the Sangha, the community of monks, has been central to Buddhism. Even today, in Buddhist Thailand, it is customary for most young men to enter a monastery, if only for a month. Meditation is also very important. In meditation Buddhists attempt to still the mind and its endless flow of thoughts, ideas, and desires, replacing them with a state of inner stillness. In this stillness, it is said, meditators become aware of their fundamental state and gain, in time, enlightenment.

Hands in meditative position

Mat for meditation

Legs crossed in half-lotus position

Tibetan Buddhism

BUDDHISM CAME TO TIBET from India in the 8th century. By that time Indian Buddhism had adapted a complicated set of rituals and "magic" from folk religion to help people to find their way to Nirvana. This branch of Buddhism was written in sacred, secret books called tantras, so it was called Tantrism. It included the use of mystic diagrams called mandalas, and sacred phrases or sayings called mantras, which disciples said over and over again. The religion that came to dominate Tibet was a mixture of Tantric and other Mahayana teachings. In Tibet, it was developed further by spiritual leaders called lamas, who are usually monks. Lamas belong to a number of different groups, or schools. These schools are based around various powerful monasteries: their ideas and practices vary, but they have usually existed in harmony. One of a lama's tasks is to guide a dying person's spirit in the time between death and rebirth. Lamas spend many years learning and meditating to gain this wisdom.

TIBET AND BEYOND
In modern times Tibetan Buddhism has had an increasing influence abroad. Tibetans and Buddhists of different traditions, such as these monks in Shanghai, are happy to share their experience and wisdom.

Vairochana, foremost of the Meditation Buddhas, perfects knowledge

Ratnasambhava, "The Beautifier", perfects goodness and beauty

Amitabha, "Infinite Compassion", perfects speech

Vajrasattva, "The Unchanging", perfects wisdom

Amoghasiddhi, "Almighty Conqueror", perfects action

THE FIVE BUDDHAS
This Tibetan lama's ritual headdress displays the "Buddhas of Meditation". According to *The Tibetan Book of the Dead*, these Buddhas dwell in the heavenly worlds. Each personifies an aspect of "Divine Being", the ultimate reality or wisdom. They meet a dead person's spirit, and the spirit's reaction shows how enlightened the person is and decides how the person will be reborn.

The demon has glaring eyes, protruding tusks, and jutting out tongue

RITUAL PROTECTION
In Indian mythology, the god Shiva creates a demon who will be the supreme destructive force of the universe. The grotesque face of this demon, called "the face of glory", is often placed on temples of Shiva as a protective device. This ritual amulet is a Tibetan adaptation of the Indian symbol and is worn to terrify demons and protect the wearer.

PRAYER WHEEL
A prayer wheel contains a mantra, a prayer or chant that is repeated many times. Each turn of the wheel counts as a prayer said and merit gained. The mantra in this prayer wheel is usually translated as "Hail to the jewel in the lotus" and is directed to Avalokiteshvara.

Chain helps wheel to spin

Mantra fits inside prayer wheel

He holds objects which illustrate Buddhist truths

As the wheel is spun, the heavy head spins fast

VENERATING RELICS
From soon after the Buddha's death, Buddhists began to collect the physical remains and belongings of holy persons and to venerate them as relics (holy objects). Here, impressions of shrines and Buddha images have been moulded from lama ashes. After the cremation of a lama, ashes are collected, mixed with clay, moulded into tablets, and placed in cases or shrines.

Bodhisattvas have graceful bodies, wear long robes and jewellery, and hold religious implements

BODHISATTVA OF COMPASSION
The story is told of how Avalokiteshvara, the Bodhisattva of Compassion, vowed to save all conscious beings, but soon became so overwhelmed by the task that his head split into a thousand pieces. The pieces were put back together again to form eleven heads, looking in all directions. With these heads and a thousand arms, nowhere is out of reach of his love and mercy. In China he is Kuan Yin, and in Japan Kannon, Goddess of Love and Mercy. In Tibet today he becomes reincarnate in the person of the Dalai Lama, now in exile but still the leading lama and Tibet's most important leader.

This Avalokiteshvara stands on a lotus-flower throne which rises on a stalk out of swirling waters

YOUNG LAMAS
Tibetan Buddhism has had a strong spiritual and moral influence on Tibetans. Since the Communist takeover of 1950, monasteries have been destroyed and the influence of religion has weakened. Many do still practise their devotions, however, and a strong movement continues among refugees. Here, young lamas blow horns as part of a monastic ritual.

When the breath has ceased… the Knower will be experiencing the Clear Light of the natural condition

THE TIBETAN BOOK OF THE DEAD, 1.i

This gilt bronze statue was made in the 18th century

Confucian piety

CONFUCIUS
Confucius, or K'ung Fu-tzu, (551–479 BCE) was China's first great philosopher. His name means "Master King"; a legend says that when he was born it was foretold that he would be "a king without a crown". His discussions and sayings are collected together in *The Analects*.

FOR MANY, CONFUCIANISM is a way of life, a code of behaviour, rather than a religion. Confucians may combine following their master, Confucius, with belief in any god or none. Confucius stressed the importance of li, which means proper or orderly conduct. He taught his followers to be "gentlemen". A gentleman is always courteous, fair, respectful to his superiors, and kind to ordinary people. He also practises "filial piety" – his duty to respect and care for his parents. Because of his belief in filial piety Confucius supported the ancient practice of venerating (giving great respect and honour to) ancestors. He wished to bring order and harmony to society, with everyone doing their duty. He taught that worshipping God and the spirits and honouring one's ancestors means nothing unless the service of other people comes first.

THE THREE WAYS
China is the land of the "Three Ways", Confucianism, Taoism, and Buddhism. For more than two thousand years, they have all played a major role in Chinese life and thought. Confucianism emphasized order and respect, Taoism provided a mystical understanding of the world, and Buddhism offered salvation through compassion and devotion. As they have developed they have merged with each other, and with the age-old folk religion of China, centred on home and family. This painting symbolically shows how the Three Ways mix by representing their three founders together: Buddha (left), Confucius (centre), and Lao-tzu (right).

CONFUCIUS DAY CEREMONY
Confucius did not try to found a religion, but to teach a way of life based on rules of good behaviour. However, after his death, shrines were built in his honour, and Confucianism became the state religion of China.

Modern Confucian temple at Taipei in Taiwan

Priests honour Confucius Day

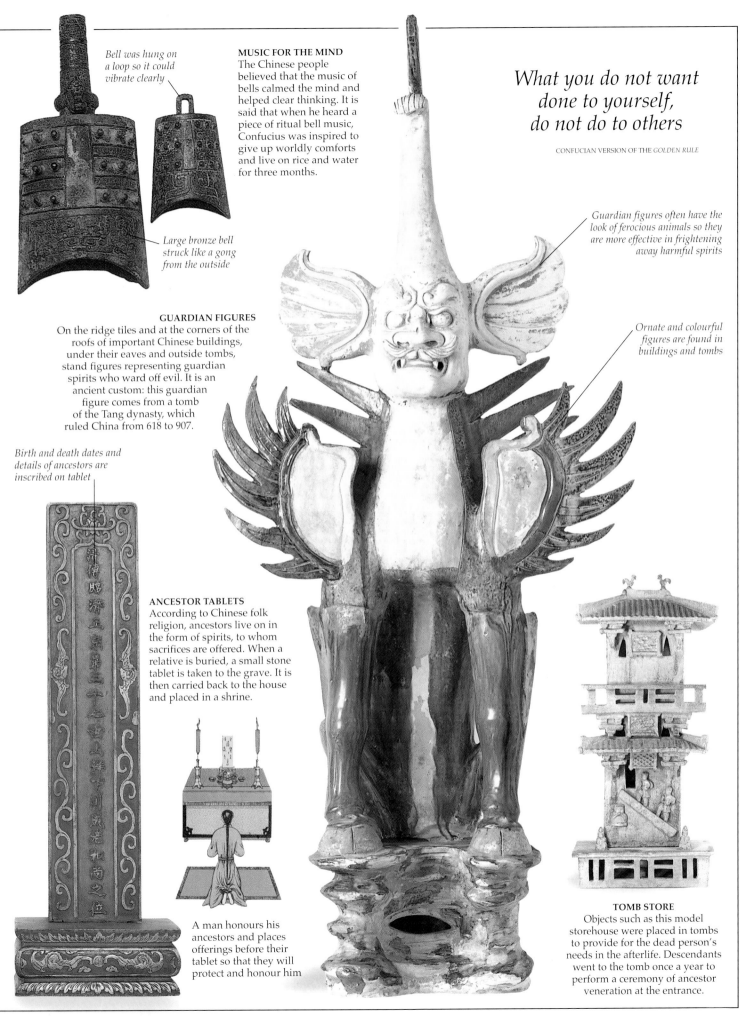

Bell was hung on a loop so it could vibrate clearly

MUSIC FOR THE MIND
The Chinese people believed that the music of bells calmed the mind and helped clear thinking. It is said that when he heard a piece of ritual bell music, Confucius was inspired to give up worldly comforts and live on rice and water for three months.

Large bronze bell struck like a gong from the outside

Guardian figures often have the look of ferocious animals so they are more effective in frightening away harmful spirits

GUARDIAN FIGURES
On the ridge tiles and at the corners of the roofs of important Chinese buildings, under their eaves and outside tombs, stand figures representing guardian spirits who ward off evil. It is an ancient custom: this guardian figure comes from a tomb of the Tang dynasty, which ruled China from 618 to 907.

Ornate and colourful figures are found in buildings and tombs

Birth and death dates and details of ancestors are inscribed on tablet

ANCESTOR TABLETS
According to Chinese folk religion, ancestors live on in the form of spirits, to whom sacrifices are offered. When a relative is buried, a small stone tablet is taken to the grave. It is then carried back to the house and placed in a shrine.

A man honours his ancestors and places offerings before their tablet so that they will protect and honour him

TOMB STORE
Objects such as this model storehouse were placed in tombs to provide for the dead person's needs in the afterlife. Descendants went to the tomb once a year to perform a ceremony of ancestor veneration at the entrance.

31

The Tao principle

TAOISTS BELIEVE THAT THERE IS a principle, or force, running through the whole of the natural world, and controlling it. They call this principle the Tao. Tao means way, or path. To follow the Tao is to follow the way of nature. It is sometimes called the "watercourse way" because Taoists see water as a picture of the Tao at work. Water is soft and yielding, it flows effortlessly to humble places, yet it is also the most powerful of substances, and it nourishes all life. There are two kinds of Taoism: the popular and the philosophical. The followers of philosophical Taoism are likely to be mystical and peaceful. By stilling the inner self, their senses and appetites, they gain an understanding of the Tao, and try to live in oneness and harmony with it. The focus of popular Taoism is different. It includes very many gods, goddesses, and spiritual beings, whose help believers seek, and demons, who are feared. Its followers use magic and ritual to harness Te – virtue or power – in the hope of becoming immortal.

YIN AND YANG
The Yin-Yang symbol represents the two halves of the Tao, the two opposite, complementary principles Taoists see in nature: Yin – dark, female, passive, soft; and Yang – light, male, active, hard.

Lu Tung-pin overcame a series of temptations and was given a magic sword, with which he killed dragons and fought evil

Li Ti'eh-kuai used to go in spirit to visit Lao-tzu in the celestial regions; he once stayed so long that his body had gone when he came back, so his spirit had to enter the body of a lame beggar

Ho Hsien-ku lived on powdered mother-of-pearl and moonbeams; her emblem is the lotus

THE FOUNDER
According to Taoist tradition, Lao-tzu lived in central China in the 6th century BCE, at the same time as Confucius, who is said to have visited him as a young man. Lao-tzu worked as keeper of archives for the Chou dynasty. In later life, tired of Chou corruption, he tried to flee to Tibet. But he was stopped at the border and refused permission to leave unless he left behind a record of his teachings. In three days he produced the *Tao Te Ching*, the greatest of Taoist writings. Then he handed it over and rode away on a water buffalo, never to be heard of again.

Ts'ao Kuo-chiu, patron of the theatre, wears a court headdress and official robes, and holds his emblem, a pair of castanets, in one hand

THE EIGHT IMMORTALS
The Eight Immortals are legendary beings believed to have attained immortality, through their practice of the Tao principle. They are said to have lived on earth at various times, and each represents a different condition in life: poverty, wealth, aristocracy, low social status, age, youth, masculinity, and femininity. Here they are shown with a fabulous being called Si Wang Mu who has the power to give away the peaches of immortality, which grow on the peach tree of the genii, beside the Lake of Gems in the West.

THE FAIRY CRANE

The traditional Chinese focus on death, immortality, and the ancestors means that funerals, and the rituals surrounding them, are often very important. A paper fairy crane is often carried at the head of the funeral procession of priests (shown here, with the abbot in his chair). The crane symbolizes a winged messenger from heaven, and when the paper crane is burnt the departed soul rides to heaven on the winged messenger's back.

To exist means to embrace the Yang principle (of the light) and turn one's back on the Yin (of the dark)

TAO TE CHING

Chang Kuo-lao, a magician, could make himself invisible

The magical being Si Wang Mu, here shown as male, more often appears as female

Han Hsiang-tzu is patron of musicians; his emblem is the flute

Chung-li Ch'uan holds a fan with which he revives the souls of the dead

Lan Ts'ai-ho, patron of florists, holds aloft her emblem, the flower-basket

GOD OF LONGEVITY

Chinese people see long life as a very desirable blessing. Therefore Shou-lai, god of longevity, is a popular deity. He is often depicted, either alone or with the Eight Immortals. His image may be carved in wood and stone, cast in bronze and porcelain, or used as a motif in embroidery and porcelain-painting. He is easily identified by his high, bulging forehead and bald head.

RITUAL POWER

Popular Taoism provides for everyday religious needs. Whatever the official philosophy, belief in personal gods and personalized spirits persists, and people still seek their help. Here priests burn incense at a popular ceremony where power (Te) is harnessed through magic and ritual. Priests are mainly concerned with cures for sickness and disease and with the casting out of evil spirits.

Shinto harmony

SACRED GATE
Since ancient times, Shinto shrines have been marked by entrance gates called torii. Because a beautiful natural setting, such as a sacred open space among trees or rocks, was often sufficient as a shrine, torii stood in such places. The great red torii to the famous island shrine of Itsukushima stands in the waters of the Inland Sea and is one of the great sights of Japan.

SHINTO IS THE MOST ANCIENT religion of Japan. The name means "the way of the gods". It is a religion of nature, focused on kami, which are supernatural spirits, or gods, in which the force of nature is concentrated. They include seas and mountains; animals, birds, and plants; even ancestors have the powers of kami. It is said there are eight million kami, worshipped at national, local, and household shrines all over Japan. The force of nature itself is also called kami, and is seen as divine. It inspires a feeling of awe and wonder. The most important shrines are associated with places of natural beauty: on the mountains, in the forests, and near the sea.

SHINTO GODDESS
Kami are rarely represented in the form of images to be worshipped. One exception is Nakatsu-hime, goddess of the Eight-Island Country directly below heaven. In one cult she is seen as an incarnation of the Buddhist goddess Kannon.

The god called Hand Strength Male approaching the cave to bring out the Sun Goddess

The gods decked out the tree of heaven with jewels and a mirror, then made music and danced to attract Amaterasu's attention

THE SUN GODDESS AMATERASU
Amaterasu Omikami, the sun goddess, is the supreme Shinto god. Her shrine at Ise is the most popular in Japan. One myth tells that her brother the Storm god made her so angry that she hid in a cave, bringing darkness to the earth. To persuade her to come out the other gods hung jewels and a mirror on the tree of heaven and danced for her. She looked out to see what was happening, saw herself in the mirror and, while watching, fascinated, was pulled outside. Since then, dawn has always followed night.

MOUNT FUJI
Since ancient times, mountains have been seen as special dwelling places of the gods. Much Shinto art deals with sacred mountains, figures, cults, shrines, settings, or themes. Shinto art also reflects the long interaction between Shinto and Buddhism.

HOLINESS

What is "holy" is separate and different, something "other" – far beyond the ordinary. Either beings or places may be holy or sacred. When we experience the holy, we feel awe and wonder, or blessing, or dread, or peace, or a sense of "wholeness". The word "holiness" also refers to moral or spiritual goodness.

SHINTO AND BUDDHISM

Shinto is more a religion of experience than of doctrine (set beliefs), so it easily blended with Buddhism after Buddhism reached Japan in the sixth century. The kami were often seen as local manifestations of buddhas and boddhisattvas, and Buddhist temples existed beside, or inside, Shinto shrines. Buddhist monks such as those above still take part in the great Shinto festivals.

Mallet to grant wishes

SHRINES AND FESTIVALS

Festivals are important in Shinto practice as the time when all a shrine's worshippers focus on it. One of the greatest is the Gion Festival, held annually since the 16th century. Local people decorate and wheel tall floats through the streets of Kyoto. During the festival this young boy pays his respects to his local god.

Boy taking part in the Gion festival

> *Wherever the "energy"*
> *of the universe attains*
> *a particular intensity,*
> *revealing itself as*
> *beauty, power, wonder,*
> *there the ultimate becomes*
> *apparent: there is "kami"*

FOSCO MARAINI IN *JAPAN: PATTERNS OF CONTINUITY*

The god Daikoku, one of the seven gods of fortune

The god's rat attendant

Sack of rice

THE SEVEN GODS

The seven gods of fortune, or good luck, were originally Buddhist deities and are now worshipped in Shinto too – another example of how Buddhism and Shinto mix. Daikoku is the god of wealth and patron of farmers. He is often pictured with his son, Ebisu, god of honest labour. He is usually shown sitting on sacks of rice, with a bag of jewels on his shoulder, a golden sun disk on his chest, and a mallet with which he grants wishes. His attendant is a rat, sometimes shown nibbling away at the rice sacks. Daikoku is rich though, and always good humoured about it. He is also said to be fond of children.

Jain respect for life

JAINISM IS AN ANCIENT INDIAN RELIGION. Its most distinctive doctrine is its belief in ahimsa, or non-violence to living things, which has influenced many non-Jains, including Mahatma Gandhi. Jains believe that the universe has neither beginning nor end – there is no creator god. The universe passes through a never-ending number of cosmic cycles. Each cycle is divided into periods of ascent and descent, during which civilization rises then falls. Tirthankaras (ford-makers) appear; there are 24 in each cycle. They first of all conquer their own passions and emotions, thus liberating and perfecting themselves, and then guide others across the "river of transmigration" (the journey of the soul from one life to the next). Jains believe that the final Tirthankara of the present period was Mahavira, founder of Jainism. Tirthankaras are also called Jinas (conquerors) – the word from which Jains take their name.

Right knowledge comes through keeping the Jain creed, right faith through believing it, and right conduct through following it

THE BIRTH OF MAHAVIRA
Vardhamana Mahavira was the 24th and last Tirthankara. Born around 540 BCE, he was brought up as a prince, but at the age of 28 he gave up everything to seek liberation from the endless round of birth-death-rebirth. He became a beggar and an ascetic (a person who lives a life of self-denial). At about the age of forty he achieved full enlightenment. He devoted the rest of his life to spreading his beliefs and organizing a community of followers.

TOTAL DETACHMENT
The inner shrine of a Jain temple is dominated by a principal image of the Tirthankara to whom the temple is dedicated. It is usually flanked by two attendants and surrounded by smaller images of the remaining 23 Tirthankaras. Here, the 20th Tirthankara sits in passionless detachment for Jains to contemplate.

These diamond- or pear-shaped marks are often shown on Tirthankaras and are good omens

Each Tirthankara has a symbol, in this case the tortoise

PARSHVA
Parshva, the 23rd Tirthankara, was a famous teacher who lived in and around Varanasi, India, about 850 BCE. Here, he is shown flanked on either side by his two attendants, and surrounded by other Tirthankaras. Above his head is a canopy formed by the seven-headed cobra Ananta, "the endless", who guards him.

Pilgrims bathing the 18-m (60-ft) high stone image of the hero Gomateshvara with turmeric

FESTIVALS

Festivals play an important part in Jain life. They may be solemn like Pajjusana, which closes the Jain year, or joyful like Divali, the great Hindu festival which has been adapted in honour of Mahavira's liberation and enlightenment.

DEITIES IN JAINISM

Jains do not worship gods, they contemplate Tirthankaras. That is the theory. In practice, however, many ordinary Jains pray to Hindu deities, and many Jain temples contain images of minor Hindu gods and goddesses. Among the most popular is Sarasvati, goddess of wisdom and the arts.

Sarasvati holds symbolic objects in her hands; the prayer beads in her upper left hand show her piety

The five seated figures around Sarasvati are Tirthankaras

As goddess of wisdom and writing, she holds a palm-leaf manuscript (now broken)

Two fly-whisk holders fan Sarasvati

The two donors are shown kneeling before the goddess

RENUNCIATION

The Jain monk is a homeless wanderer. He owns hardly anything except his robes, pieces of cloth with which to strain insects away when he drinks, and a brush with which to sweep insects from the path before him, so as not to hurt them.

NON-VIOLENCE

Non-violence, or ahimsa, is the principle of not inflicting harm on others, particularly human beings. For some, particularly Jains, the idea is extended to any living thing. Non-violence starts with an attitude of mind. It is against harmful thoughts as well as aggressive deeds.

Sikh teaching

Sikhs can be found in almost every part of the world. Their gurdwaras (temples) adorn the cities of Britain, East Africa, Malaysia, the west coast of Canada, and the United States. The vast majority, however, live in India. Their founder, Guru Nanak, was born in the Punjab in 1469. Nanak taught a new doctrine of salvation, centring on two basic ideas, one about the nature of God, one about the nature of humankind. To Sikhs, God is single and personal. He is the Creator with whom the individual must develop the most intimate of relationships. People are wilfully blind; they shut their eyes to this divine revelation and need a guru (a spiritual guide) to teach them. The idea of the guru lies at the heart of the Sikh religion: even the name "Sikh" comes from an old word meaning "disciple". After Nanak, there were nine more gurus. The last guru passed his authority to the community and to the Sikh holy book.

THE SIKH STANDARD
The Sikh emblem, the nishan sahib, contains a ring of steel representing the unity of God, a two-edged sword symbolizing God's concern for truth and justice, and two crossed, curved swords around the outside to signify God's spiritual power. A flag with the nishan sahib on it is flown from every gurdwara (Sikh temple).

THE GOLDEN TEMPLE
The Golden Temple at Amritsar is the central shrine of Sikhism, and its most important place of pilgrimage. On entering, pilgrims offer coins and each receives a small portion of karah parshad (holy food which symbolizes equality and brotherhood). They then sit and listen to the singing of passages from the scriptures. The water surrounding the temple is considered especially holy and pilgrims often bathe in it.

Silk cloth placed over cover of holy book

FOCUS OF WORSHIP
Gurdwara literally means "the door of the guru" and the temple houses the holy scriptures, called the Guru Granth Sahib. The scriptures contain spiritual poetry written by the ten gurus. The Granth is the supreme authority for Sikhs and Sikh worship centres on its guidance. The book is greatly revered; it is placed on a cushion under a canopy and covered with a silk cloth in the main body of the temple.

Even when the pages of the Granth are being read, its cover is covered with silk cloths (not shown here)

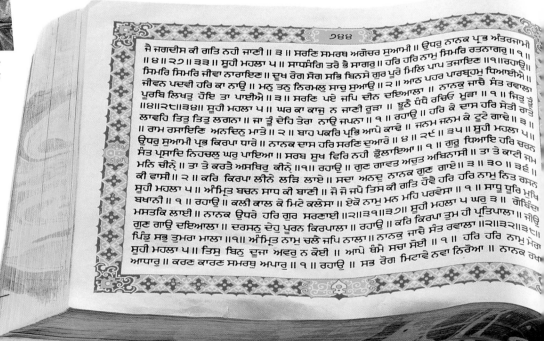

Guru Nanak, founder of the Sikh religion

The kara (steel bangle)

The kangha (comb)

THE FIVE K'S
The Khalsa (community) was founded by Gobind Singh, last of the ten gurus. Young Sikhs enter at puberty. It has five outward symbols, known as the "five K's": the sword, comb, bangle, uncut hair (with a turban worn over it), and breeches.

The other nine gurus (shown with haloes) sit around Guru Nanak

THE TEN GURUS
Sikhism is sometimes called Gurmat, meaning "the Guru's doctrine". God, the original Guru, imparted his message to his chosen disciple, Nanak, first of a series of ten gurus. Gurus were chosen by their predecessors for their spiritual insight. Gobind Singh (1666–1708) was the last. He transferred his authority to the community and the scriptures. He said that the scriptures would be their guru, so the book was called the Guru Granth Sahib.

God is One, He is the True Name, He is the Creator

THE OPENING WORDS OF THE *GURU GRANTH SAHIB*

The kirpan (sword)

The language is a mixture of Punjabi and Hindi and is sung to classical Indian chants; most of the book is poetry

SIGN OF RESPECT
The chauri or whisk is a symbol of authority and is waved over the holy book to show honour and respect for it, because a whisk would once have been waved over a human guru in the Punjab (to keep the flies away), and the book is now the guru. The chauri can be made of peacock feathers, yak hair, goat hair or, as here, synthetic material.

THE GURU GRANTH SAHIB
The Guru Granth Sahib is a collection of the teachings of Guru Nanak and the other gurus. At the beginning are a number of verses attributed to Nanak himself, and these are recited by Sikhs in their morning prayers. Next come poems and hymns which are attributed to various gurus and always sung. Central to the scriptures is the idea of salvation. A Sikh is awakened by the divine guru and, through meditation on the divine Name and hearing the divine Word, the disciple ultimately unites with the divine harmony.

Zoroastrianism

ON THE EXTREME EDGE of the western Iranian desert, in and around Bombay in India, in East Africa, and in many of the major cities of the world are pockets of a small community totalling no more than 130,000 members worldwide. They are the Zoroastrians, known in India as the Parsis or "Persians", followers of the prophet Zoroaster, who lived in ancient Persia. Zoroaster called for people to live the "good life" and follow Ahura Mazda, the "Supreme Creator", or "Wise Lord", symbolized by fire. Zoroaster believed that the world was essentially good, though tainted by evil. He also believed that, just as Ahura Mazda is responsible for all the good in life, so misery and suffering are the work of an independent force of evil, Angra Mainyu. The two powers are locked in conflict. It is the duty of all people to support the good. Those who choose good are rewarded with happiness. Those who choose evil end in sorrow. Zoroaster taught that in the end good would triumph over evil.

GUARDIAN SPIRIT
Zoroastrians see this image as a fravashi, a guardian spirit. They say that everyone is watched over by a fravashi. Fravashis represent the good, or the God-essence, in people. They help those who ask them and work for good in the universe. This symbol can also be seen as representing "the spiritual self", or Ahura Mazda. It is found very often in Zoroastrianism.

DRINK OF IMMORTALITY
The ritual most associated with Zoroastrians is that of tending the sacred fire. In the major ceremony of Yasna, a prayer ceremony, the sacred liquor haoma (made of the juice of a plant) is offered to the sacred fire. The offering and drinking of this consecrated juice confers immortality on the worshipper.

Mask over face because sacred objects would be contaminated if sneezed on

THE AGE OF RESPONSIBILITY
Before puberty, between the ages of seven and twelve, young Zoroastrians are initiated into their faith in the Navjote ceremony, at which they symbolically take on the responsibility to uphold the ideas and morals of Zoroastrianism. They are given a sacred thread, or kushti, to wear, and a sacred vest, or sudreh. The vest is white, for purity and renewal. The 72 strands of the thread symbolize a universal fellowship.

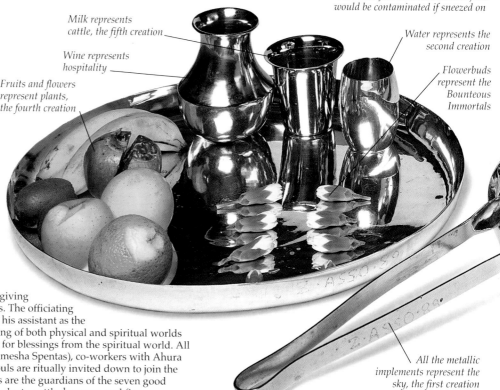

Milk represents cattle, the fifth creation

Wine represents hospitality

Fruits and flowers represent plants, the fourth creation

Water represents the second creation

Flowerbuds represent the Bounteous Immortals

All the metallic implements represent the sky, the first creation

THANKSGIVING CEREMONY
A Jashan is a ceremony of thanksgiving performed by two or more priests. The officiating priest is known as the zaotar and his assistant as the raspi. Jashan ensures the well-being of both physical and spiritual worlds as the living offer thanks and ask for blessings from the spiritual world. All seven "Bounteous Immortals" (Amesha Spentas), co-workers with Ahura Mazda, and departed virtuous souls are ritually invited down to join the Jashan. The Bounteous Immortals are the guardians of the seven good creations – the sky, waters, earth, plants, cattle, humans, and fire – represented symbolically by the materials and implements used.

THE FOUNDER

Zoroaster or, more correctly, Zarathusthra in ancient Persian, is commonly believed to have lived between 1500 and 1000 BCE, which would make him the earliest known of the great prophets of the world's religions. Little is known about his life, except that he was a priest as well as being a prophet and was married with several children. The religion he founded was for more than a thousand years the official religion of Persia (now Iran), one of the world's greatest empires.

Afarganyu (fire-vase); sandalwood burns continuously on it to represent God, the source of light and life

FIRE TEMPLE

Originally, Zoroastrian worship was conducted in the open air. Nowadays, however, every Zoroastrian community worships in a fire temple where prayer rituals are performed in the presence of a sacred fire, which is seen as a living embodiment of Ahura Mazda. No images are allowed, and only Zoroastrians may enter the temple. Before entering, worshippers wash their hands and faces and then perform the kushti prayer ritual. Then they slip off their shoes to enter the fire temple to present themselves before the fire. They apply a pinch of ash from the sacred fire to their foreheads, then pray, focusing on the pure light of Ahura Mazda.

Good thoughts, good words, good deeds

THE ZOROASTRIAN IDEAL

Tray of sandalwood and frankincense

The traditional oil lamp which is kept burning

Flat circular spoon used by the raspi (assistant priest) to offer sandalwood and frankincense to the fire

The Jewish nation

T HE JEWISH PEOPLE trace their ancestry back to three ancient leaders known as the patriarchs: Abraham, his son Isaac, and his grandson Jacob. In their daily prayers, Jews still call themselves "children of Abraham". They call their nation Israel because God re-named Jacob, Israel. Their story began when Abraham left what is now Iraq in about 1800 BCE to settle in Canaan, the "Promised Land", now known as Palestine or Israel. Later, Jacob's sons went to Egypt. Around 1250 BCE, their descendants, the Hebrews, were led out by Moses, in the journey known as the Exodus. On the way the God of the patriarchs appeared to Moses on Mount Sinai and made a covenant (agreement) with Israel. It was enshrined in the Ten Commandments, and later in the rest of the Torah, the "law of Moses". Ever since, this God-given religious law has been at the heart of Israel's identity as a people. Jews see God as both the God of Israel, his "chosen people", and also the creator and ruler of all that is, the God who controls history, all-powerful and all-loving.

CROSSING THE RED SEA
According to the Bible, the descendants of Jacob's twelve sons, the twelve tribes of Israel, became slaves in Egypt. Eventually, God called Moses to lead them out of slavery. God had to send ten plagues on Egypt before Pharaoh would let them go. Even then, Pharaoh changed his mind and sent his army to trap them by the Red Sea. God parted the sea for the Israelites. When the Egyptians tried to cross, the sea closed over them. This is one of the events celebrated at the annual Passover festival. In such festivals, the history of the Jewish people is kept alive, and the lessons it has taught them about God are remembered.

THE WESTERN WALL
The Western Wall is all that remains of the second Temple, built by King Herod, that stood in Jerusalem 2,000 years ago, when Jerusalem was the capital of the ancient Jewish kingdom. The Temple was the centre of Jewish worship until it was destroyed by the Romans in 70 CE, after which the Jews were scattered and did not have their own state for 1,900 years. The wall is a symbol of the Temple and a memorial of its destruction. It is the holiest site for Jews in Jerusalem.

A BABY BOY
When God made a covenant with Abraham, he commanded that all boys born into Abraham's people should be circumcised as a sign of God's choice of Israel as his chosen people. They are circumcised still, eight days after birth. This is a cloth made for a baby boy.

The wall used to be called the Wailing Wall because it was associated with crying for the destruction of the Temple

Jewish people come from all over the world to pray at the wall

The Hebrew reads "May he live for the Torah, the Huppah, and good deeds"

The Huppah or Wedding Canopy, the indispensable covering for the bridal pair during the marriage ceremony

The Torah or scroll of the Law

שְׁמַע יִשְׂרָאֵל יְהוָה אֱלֹהֵינוּ יְהוָה אֶחָד וְאָהַבְתָּ אֵת יְהוָה אֱלֹהֶיךָ בְּכָל לְבָבְךָ וּבְכָל נַפְשְׁךָ וּבְכָל מְאֹדֶךָ וְהָיוּ הַדְּבָרִים הָאֵלֶּה אֲשֶׁר אָנֹכִי מְצַוְּךָ הַיּוֹם עַל לְבָבֶךָ וְשִׁנַּנְתָּם לְבָנֶיךָ וְדִבַּרְתָּ בָּם בְּשִׁבְתְּךָ בְּבֵיתֶךָ וּבְלֶכְתְּךָ בַדֶּרֶךְ וּבְשָׁכְבְּךָ וּבְקוּמֶךָ וּקְשַׁרְתָּם לְאוֹת עַל יָדֶךָ וְהָיוּ לְטֹטָפֹת בֵּין עֵינֶיךָ וּכְתַבְתָּם עַל מְזֻזוֹת בֵּיתֶךָ וּבִשְׁעָרֶיךָ

The first part of the biblical text of the Shema

A ninth candle, called the servant candle, is used to light the rest

The star of David, Israel's greatest king

THE MEZUZAH
The Mezuzah is a tiny parchment scroll inscribed with biblical texts and enclosed in a case. Traditionally, Mezuzahs are fixed to the door-frames of Jewish homes. They usually contain the words of the Shema from the Bible, which calls God's people to love him totally. Religious Jews repeat the Shema morning and evening because it sums up the heart of their faith.

A candle is lit for each of the eight days of the festival

Hear, O Israel: the Lord your God, the Lord is one… Love the Lord your God with all your heart, and with all your soul, and with all your might

THE BEGINNING OF THE SHEMA

HANUKKAH, FESTIVAL OF LIGHTS
Hanukkah is an eight-day midwinter festival marked by the lighting of ritual candles. It celebrates the rededication of the temple of Jerusalem by Judas Maccabeus after he had recaptured it from an enemy army in 164 BCE. The Jewish religious year includes a number of festivals, which remind Jews of God's faithfulness to his people in the past and help them to be dedicated to him.

JUDAISM

ONE GOD?
Yes

THE AFTERLIFE?
Yes, but Judaism is mainly concerned with this life

FOUNDERS?
Abraham, father of the Jewish people, lived in the Middle East c.1800 BCE
Moses, gave the Torah (the law), lived in the Middle East c.1250 BCE

SCRIPTURES?
The Jewish Bible, of which the Torah (the law of Moses) is the most important part

A WRITTEN CODE?
The Torah, which gives guidance for all aspects of life

People of the Torah

AT THE HEART of the Jewish religion is the Torah, "the Law", written in the first five books of the Hebrew Bible. Torah does not only mean "law", but also "teaching" and "guidance". In the Torah, God has given teaching about himself, his purposes, and how he wishes his people to obey him in every part of their lives. For a religious Jew, to obey the Torah is to follow God's guidance. The reading of the Torah is a major part of worship in the synagogue (assembly). People also respond to God by communicating with him in prayer. Jewish people have a special role in God's plans for humanity, since it was to them that God revealed the Torah. They look forward to a time when God will send his Messiah ("anointed one") to announce the final setting up of God's rule, or kingdom, on earth.

ARK OF THE COVENANT
The ark of the covenant holds the scrolls of the Torah. It sits behind a curtain in the synagogue wall that faces towards Jerusalem. The original ark of the covenant held the Ten Commandments while Israel journeyed from Egypt towards the Promised Land.

COMING OF AGE
When a Jewish boy reaches thirteen, he becomes Bar Mitzvah, "a son of the commandments". He is then considered to be a responsible adult, and is expected to follow all the commandments of the Law. For a girl the age of responsibility is twelve.

The Hebrew text reads "Crown of the Torah"

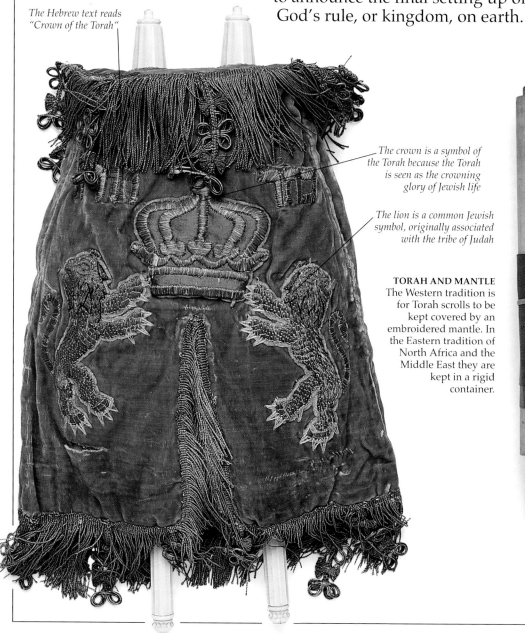

The crown is a symbol of the Torah because the Torah is seen as the crowning glory of Jewish life

The lion is a common Jewish symbol, originally associated with the tribe of Judah

TORAH AND MANTLE
The Western tradition is for Torah scrolls to be kept covered by an embroidered mantle. In the Eastern tradition of North Africa and the Middle East they are kept in a rigid container.

44

The deeper you dig into the Torah, the more treasures you uncover

ISAAC BASHEVIS SINGER

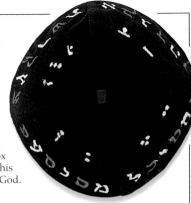

SIGN OF RESPECT
A strictly religious Jewish man prays three times a day, in the morning, afternoon, and evening, either at home or in the synagogue. When he prays he covers his head with a hat, or a skull-cap, known as yarmelka or kippah. When he goes out, an orthodox Jew may continue to cover his head as a sign of respect for God.

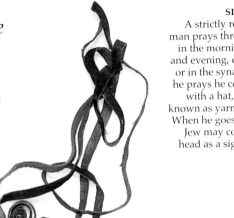

WEARING THE TORAH
During their daily prayers, Jewish men wear a pair of small black leather boxes containing passages from the Torah strapped to their upper left arms and above their foreheads. These boxes are called phylacteries, or tephillin.

Shofar (ram's horn) with Hebrew script on it

CALL TO REPENTANCE
At Rosh Hashanah (the Jewish New Year) the shofar or ram's horn is blown to call Jewish people to repentance (to ask God to forgive all the wrong things they have done in the past year). This begins the ten solemn days leading up to Yom Kippur, the Day of Atonement, a day of fasting and repentance, and the holiest day of the Jewish year.

SON OF THE TORAH
When a Jewish boy becomes Bar Mitzvah the family and community celebrate. They attend the synagogue, and during a Sabbath service, the boy will exercise his full adult rights for the first time by putting on the tallit and reading in public from the Law (the Torah) and the Prophets. The tallit is a prayer shawl with tassels at both ends, worn by Jewish men at morning prayer and on Yom Kippur. Some, but not all, synagogues also have parallel Bat Mitzvah coming of age ceremonies for girls.

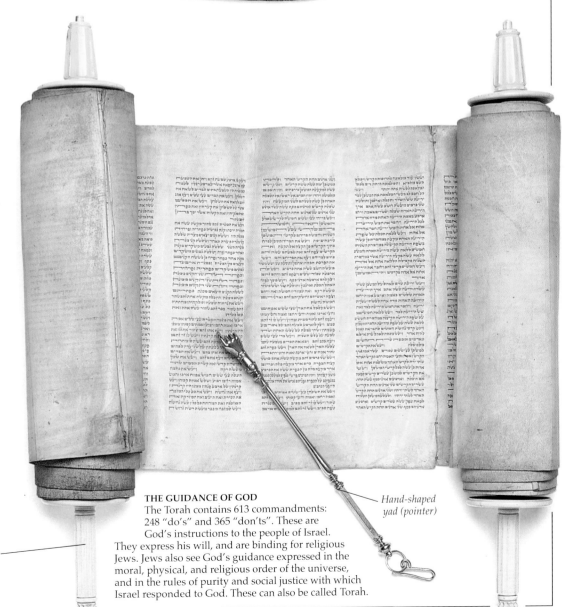

The Torah scroll is too sacred to touch, so it is held by handles and a pointer is used to keep the place

THE GUIDANCE OF GOD
The Torah contains 613 commandments: 248 "do's" and 365 "don'ts". These are God's instructions to the people of Israel. They express his will, and are binding for religious Jews. Jews also see God's guidance expressed in the moral, physical, and religious order of the universe, and in the rules of purity and social justice with which Israel responded to God. These can also be called Torah.

Hand-shaped yad (pointer)

Palm frond

Family and community

THE CENTRE OF JEWISH RELIGIOUS LIFE is the home. Great emphasis is laid on the family and relationships. The Jewish year contains many festivals, which give a pattern and a rhythm to the community's life. Many of them are not only religious, but family festivals too. These festivals bind the community together. They also make the continuing story of Israel's relationship with God a living part of people's lives. The most important is the weekly Shabbat (Sabbath), a day of rest when Jews do no work and recall the completion of creation. At the centre of public worship and of social life is the synagogue, or "assembly". On Friday evenings and on Saturday mornings the Jewish community gathers there for Sabbath services.

CUP OF BLESSING
Most Jewish homes have a wine goblet called a Kiddush cup. The name comes from the words of blessing, also called Kiddush, spoken over the wine and bread during Sabbath and the Passover.

PURIM
Nearly half-way through the Jewish year (in February or March) comes Purim which is marked by parties where masks and elaborate costumes are sometimes worn. Purim means "lots". The name refers to a time in the 5th century BCE when an official in the Persian Empire called Haman made a plan to kill all the Jews and drew lots to decide when. During the festival the Book of Esther from the Bible is read aloud to recall how Esther, the King's wife, helped save her people from slaughter.

Purim scroll containing the Book of Esther

Etrog, a citrus fruit

SUKKOT
Sukkot takes place in September or October, at the end of harvest. During this festival Jews recall how God provided for all their needs when they wandered in the wilderness after leaving Egypt. Festive huts are built, roofed with greenery and decorated with fruit and flowers. In a ceremony called the "Four Species", a lulav is carried in procession with an etrog while prayers are said.

Palm, myrtle, and willow, woven together, form the lulav

Lulav, carried in procession at Sukkot

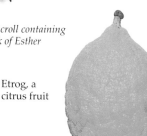

Sukkot huts are built in gardens or next to a synagogue and, if possible, people eat and sleep in them for the week of the festival

LIGHTING THE SABBATH CANDLES
The Jewish day begins and ends at sunset, so the Sabbath, which falls on a Saturday, begins on Friday evening, when the woman of a Jewish household kindles the "Sabbath Lights" and prays for God's blessing on her work and family. The Sabbath table is then laid with bread and wine. Before the meal the husband praises his wife and recites scriptures about creation and the Sabbath. Then he blesses the wine and bread and passes them round.

PASSOVER

The week-long Passover is the best known of all Jewish festivals. It is held to commemorate the events related in the Book of Exodus in the Torah. The festival is called Passover because, when God sent a final punishment on Egypt to persuade Pharaoh to let his people go, the angel of death "passed over" the Hebrews and spared them. At the Passover meal the youngest child in the family asks why this night is different from all other nights. The father tells the story of Israel's deliverance from slavery in Egypt (the Exodus). He tells of the harshness of life in Egypt, of Moses who led the Jewish people out of slavery, of how God gave Moses the Ten Commandments, and how God looked after Israel in the desert.

The Haggadah (meaning "Storytelling") is the special order of service for the Passover meal

Egg symbolizes sacrifice

Shankbone of lamb recalls lambs killed at the first Passover

Cloth with which the unleavened bread is covered when not being eaten

The word Pesach, Hebrew for Passover

Vegetable representing spring

Nut and fruit paste

Bitter herbs to represent the bitterness of slavery

Salt water, as a reminder of the tears of slavery

The special meal held in the home on the first two nights of Passover is called Seder (order); these dishes are placed on the table to teach the Passover story

Matzah (bread made without yeast) recalls the haste with which the Israelites left Egypt

CONTEMPLATION

To contemplate is to think about something or to gaze upon an object. Religious people practise quiet reflection and focused prayer, concentrating their minds on God, or on some other reality which transcends (rises above) the self. By this means they can experience oneness or "union" with the divine.

The Christian faith

CHRISTIANS TAKE THEIR NAME from Jesus Christ. Jesus was a Jew who lived in the first century in what is now Israel. At the age of 30 he gathered a band of disciples and travelled about preaching, teaching, and healing the sick. He declared the need for people to repent (ask for forgiveness for their sins), and to believe and follow him. His disciples saw Jesus as the Messiah the Jews expected. For Christians, Jesus is not just a man. They believe that God, creator and ruler of the universe, became incarnate (came to earth as a human being) in Christ to offer forgiveness and salvation to humankind. This was necessary, Christians believe, because God is good and people are not, which creates a gap or barrier between humanity and God. Christians see Jesus as the saviour (rescuer) who brings people to God.

JOHN THE BAPTIST
At the time of Jesus' birth, many Jews were expecting a prophet to come as a "forerunner" heralding the coming of the Messiah. John began teaching before Jesus did, preaching a baptism of repentance for the forgiveness of sins. When Jesus was 30, John baptized him in the River Jordan, after which Jesus began to teach and preach. Christians believe that John came to prepare the way for Jesus, and baptism has always been the sign of a person's entry into the Christian community.

SIGN OF THE CROSS
Jesus was executed by being nailed to a cross and left to die (this is called crucifixion). The cross later became the main symbol of Christianity because Christians believe that Christ actually brought salvation by his death and resurrection. When people become Christians and are baptized, they are marked with the sign of the cross.

The crown shows Mary as the Queen of Heaven

THE HOLY TRINITY
This picture is used by many Christians to help them think about the Christian belief that God is Trinity. This means that there are three persons in God – the Father, the Son, and the Holy Spirit – yet at the same time God is one. In the second person of the Trinity, Jesus, God became human. In the third person, the Holy Spirit, God continues to be present on earth.

VIRGIN AND CHILD
There are statues of Jesus with his mother Mary, such as this one, in many Christian churches. Respect for Mary as "mother of God" has developed steadily in some (though not all) branches of Christianity. She is called "the Blessed Virgin Mary" because Christians believe that Jesus's father was not a man, but God. Many Christians have great reverence for Mary and ask her to pray for them from heaven.

CHRISTIANITY

ONE GOD?
Yes: one god in three persons – Father, Son, and Holy Spirit – the Trinity

THE AFTERLIFE?
A final judgement, followed by heaven or hell

FOUNDER?
Jesus Christ, who lived in Palestine c.6 BCE–30 CE

SCRIPTURES?
The Bible, made up of the Old Testament (the Jewish Bible) and the New Testament

MAJOR FESTIVALS?
Christmas – Jesus' birthday
Easter – His death and resurrection

PRIESTS?
Most churches have priests

THE CHRISTMAS STORY

The most familiar image of the Christian story is of Christ's nativity (birth), which Christians celebrate at Christmas. In this picture, Jesus, Mary, and her husband Joseph are surrounded by the animals who lived in the stable, local shepherds and their sheep, and angels. The angels are singing "Glory to God in the highest heaven, and on earth peace among those whom he favours" as they rejoice at the birth of Christ, the "Prince of Peace". Jesus was born at Bethlehem in Judea (southern Israel) and brought up at Nazareth in Galilee in northern Israel. His mother Mary and Joseph, although poor, were descended from Israel's most famous king, King David.

I am the light of the world. Whoever follows me will never walk in darkness but will have the light of life

JESUS IN *JOHN* 8: 12

God the Father watches from heaven, holding the world in his hand and worshipped by angels

Angels announce the birth to surprised local shepherds

Picture showing the story of Christ's birth, from a 15th-century book

The baby Jesus was born in a stable because there was no room at the inn in Bethlehem

Mary and Joseph dressed in blue, the colour of divinity and heaven

The painting shows the dress and styles of the time when it was painted

Way of the cross

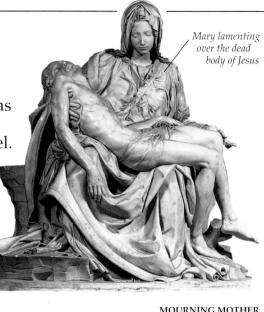

Mary lamenting over the dead body of Jesus

At the age of thirty-three, Jesus was arrested, tortured, and crucified by the Roman authorities who then ruled Israel. Christians believe that as he died he "took on himself" the sins of everyone (all the wrong and evil that, Christians say, is in us and cuts us off from God) so that anyone could be forgiven by God and live with God forever. Three days later, according to the Bible, he rose from the dead. He appeared to and taught his disciples, then "ascended" to heaven, returning to his Father. So, for Christians, Christ is a living saviour who has defeated death, not a dead hero. They believe that he helps and guides those who follow him and that he makes it possible for all to share in his victory over death and sin.

CUP OF SUFFERING
Shortly before he died, Jesus held a farewell meal, the "last supper", with his disciples. He offered them wine to drink and bread to eat and told them to drink the cup and eat the bread ever afterwards to represent his blood shed and his life laid down for them. Ever since, Christians have followed this command in services called communion services, the Mass, the Eucharist, or the Lord's Supper.

MOURNING MOTHER
At the beginning of the gospel story (gospel means "good news"), Mary is asked if she is willing to be the mother of the Son of God, and agrees. This is seen as a great example of faith. Many Christians see her as uniquely blessed by God. She is not often mentioned in the Gospels, but when the time came for Jesus to die she was one of the few who did not abandon him. She is often pictured in Christian art. A sculpture or picture showing her mourning over the dead body of her son (as above) is called a pieta.

THE CRUCIFIXION OF CHRIST
Outside the city of Jerusalem Jesus was put to death with two criminals. He carried the cross on which he was to be executed to the place of his death. Crucifixion was then a common, but very painful, method of execution. Christians seek to live, to love, and to accept suffering patiently as Jesus did, following him in "the way of the cross". Pictures of the crucifixion feature greatly in Christian art. This picture shows people who were actually there, and later Christians, together at the foot of the cross, showing that all of them look to the "saving death" of Christ for their salvation.

The pelican was used as a symbol of Christ because it was believed to give up its own blood to feed its young

The writing on the cross quoted Jesus as claiming to be "King of the Jews"

One criminal taunted Jesus; the other asked "Remember me when you come into your kingdom"

John, author of the fourth Gospel, whose symbol is an eagle

THE CRUCIFIX AND THE CROSS

Crucifixes show Christ hanging on the cross, and are symbols of his death and the salvation which, Christians say, it brought. Crosses are empty, and so remind Christians of his resurrection also. The four Gospels whose authors are represented on this cross are the four books in the New Testament which tell of the life, death, and resurrection of Jesus. They are said to have been written by four early Christians called Matthew, Mark, Luke, and John.

ASCETICISM

The ascetic renounces or denies many ordinary human activities and bodily comforts to live a very simple, ordered, and disciplined life. Such a life also involves dedication to regular prayer and contemplation of the divine. Ascetics may even give up home and job to follow their chosen path.

Luke, author of the third Gospel, whose symbol is an ox

Matthew, author of the first Gospel, whose symbol is a man

If we have died with Christ, we believe that we shall also live with him

ROMANS 6:8

Lambs were traditionally used for sacrifice; Christ is pictured as the "lamb of God who takes away the sins of the world" because he sacrificed himself

Mark, author of the second Gospel, whose symbol is a lion

RESURRECTION

The body of Jesus was laid in a tomb with a big stone across the entrance. When some of his women followers went to the tomb they found the stone rolled away and the tomb empty. Angels appeared and told them that Jesus had risen from the dead.

ASCENSION TO HEAVEN

After his resurrection Jesus appeared to his followers in Jerusalem and Galilee over a period of 40 days. He taught them and commanded them to tell all people the gospel ("good news") that his death had made forgiveness and new life possible for all, and to baptize people in the name of the Father, the Son, and the Holy Spirit. Then he ascended into heaven to return to God.

The marks of the nails in Jesus' hands and feet are clearly shown in this picture of him rising from his grave

Church of Christ

CHRISTIANS BELIEVE that before Jesus ascended to heaven he promised he would send the Spirit of God to be with his followers after he left them. Shortly afterwards, the Holy Spirit descended upon the disciples, who were gathered in Jerusalem, filling them with new boldness and power. They went out and preached that Jesus was the promised Messiah, calling on people to turn away from their sins and to be baptized in his name. They formed a community of faith which continues today – an assembly of baptized believers known as "the church", guided by the Holy Spirit. The early church spread rapidly from Jerusalem across the Roman empire. Today it numbers nearly two billion members worldwide. Christians see the church as "the body of Christ", united by faith in him, and called to do his work in the world. They seek to love God and other people as Jesus did, to spread his teaching, and to live as he lived.

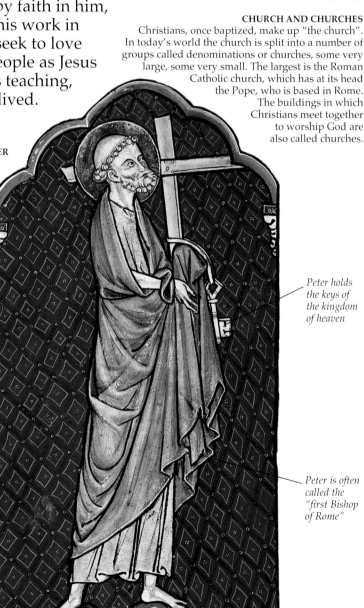

CHURCH AND CHURCHES
Christians, once baptized, make up "the church". In today's world the church is split into a number of groups called denominations or churches, some very large, some very small. The largest is the Roman Catholic church, which has at its head the Pope, who is based in Rome. The buildings in which Christians meet together to worship God are also called churches.

THE SACRAMENT OF BAPTISM
Christians celebrate the two ceremonies of baptism and communion. These ceremonies are called sacraments (some Christians believe there are also five other sacraments). Some branches of Christianity see sacraments as signs symbolizing God's inward, spiritual work; others say they are also instruments, used by God to do that work. Baptism is the rite of entry into the church; water is used, symbolizing the spiritual cleansing of the believer's soul.

PETER THE LEADER
Peter was the first disciple to recognize Jesus as the Messiah. He became the chief of the apostles ("sent ones"), the group of 12 leading disciples, and the leader of the early Christians. He is said to have gone to Rome and led the church there.

Peter holds the keys of the kingdom of heaven

Peter is often called the "first Bishop of Rome"

Christians believe the Bible to be "the Word of God", uniquely inspired by God

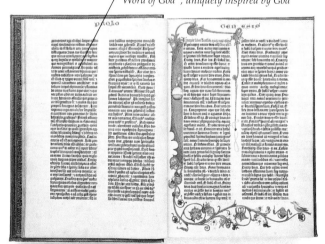

THE BIBLE
The Bible is the Christian holy book. The first part is the Jewish Bible, called the Old Testament by Christians. The second part, called the New Testament, is made up of the writings of early Christians. The Bible is seen as having unique authority.

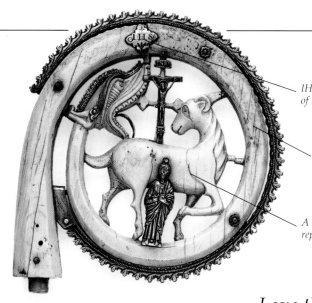

IHS, the first three letters of the Greek word for Jesus

As a sign of their authority bishops may carry a staff called a crozier, shaped like a shepherd's crook; this is the head of one such staff

A lamb near a cross, used to represent the sacrifice of Christ

Martin Luther preaching

BISHOPS AND SHEPHERDS

In the Bible Jesus is described as "the good shepherd". Christian leaders were therefore also seen as shepherds, called to look after the people in their churches as a good shepherd looks after his sheep. Early Christians who led and cared for others became known as "pastors" and their leaders as "chief pastors" or "bishops."

Love the Lord your God with all your heart... and your neighbour as yourself

MARK 12:30-31

DIFFERENT CHURCHES

By the 11th century Christianity was split into two main groups: the Roman Catholic church in western Europe, headed by the Pope in Rome, and the Eastern Orthodox, centred on Constantinople (now Istanbul) and eastern Europe. Reformers such as Luther and Calvin broke away from the authority of the Pope in the 16th century. Their followers came to be known as Protestants.

PREACHING AND TEACHING

Jesus spent much of his time preaching and teaching. He taught both by sermons and by parables – little stories, taken from ordinary life, with a spiritual meaning. The best known of Jesus' sermons is "The Sermon on the Mount", shown here. Jesus' parables and sermons are recorded in the Bible and are still used today to teach and to spread the Christian faith.

The twelve apostles listen to the sermon

Jesus Christ preaching

The message of Islam

ISLAM IS A RELIGION of submission. Its followers, Muslims, are "those who commit themselves in surrender to the will of Allah" (Allah is the Arabic word for God). The word "Islam" itself means "commitment" or "surrender". Muslims see their faith as God's final revelation, which meets all the spiritual and religious needs of humanity. The religion began with the Prophet Muhammad, who was born in the city of Mecca in Arabia, in about 571. At about the age of 40 he found that he was being called to become a prophet and preach the message of the one true God. At first, he met much opposition and in 622 he left Mecca with his followers for the nearby city of Medina. By 630 he had made them into a powerful religious and political community and was able to re-enter Mecca in triumph.

THE CRESCENT
The crescent, seen on top of many mosques, originally signified the waxing moon. It is associated with special acts of devotion to God. The star and crescent appear on the flags of countries that are mainly Muslim.

SACRED TEXTS
Calligraphy (the art of writing) in Arabic is a great Islamic art. Wherever possible Muslims try to learn Arabic because God revealed his Word to Muhammad in Arabic, and they wish to read it in the original language. The writing on this tile is a fragment from the Qur'an.

The mihrab in the Gila Khalina mosque

THE KA'BAH AT MECCA
The great mosque in Mecca is built around the Ka'bah. Set into the wall of the Ka'bah is the Black Stone, which Muslims believe fell from heaven as a sign of the first covenant between God and humankind.

PILGRIMAGE TO MECCA
The Ka'bah is Islam's most sacred site. Every Muslim who is healthy, free from debt, and can afford the journey must make the pilgrimage to Mecca at least once in his lifetime, to visit the Ka'bah and other sacred sites. Pilgrimage is the fifth of the five pillars (or duties) of Islam. The others are: first, confession of faith; second, prayer; third, fasting during the month of Ramadan; and, fourth, charitable giving. The duties are based on the Qur'an, and the practices of the Prophet Muhammad.

PRAYING TOWARDS MECCA
Prayer is the second of the five pillars of Islam. Muslims are required to pray five times a day, facing Mecca – in the morning, at noon, mid-afternoon, after sunset, and at bedtime. In every mosque there is a niche in the wall called a mihrab which faces towards Mecca to show people which way they should turn as they pray.

DOME OF THE ROCK
The Dome of the Rock, with its gilded dome and octagonal base, stands in Jerusalem. After the Great Mosque at Mecca and the Prophet's tomb at Medina, it is Islam's third holiest site. According to Muslim tradition, the rock at its centre was the point from which the Prophet Muhammad miraculously visited heaven one night in 619. The site is also sacred to Jews and Christians, because the temples of Solomon and Herod stood here.

ISLAM

ONE GOD?
Yes, Allah, the merciful and compassionate

THE AFTERLIFE?
A last judgement, followed by heaven or hell

FOUNDER OR PROPHET?
The Prophet Muhammad, lived in Arabia c.571–632

SCRIPTURES?
The Qur'an, revealed to Muhammad

PRIESTS?
None

HOLIEST PLACE?
The Ka'bah at Mecca in Arabia

The words of the shahadah are woven into the curtain covering the walls of the Ka'bah

The Ka'bah is a cube-like building made of grey stone; the Black Stone is set into its eastern corner, on the outside

There is no god but God, and Muhammad is the Prophet of God

THE SHAHADAH (THE CONFESSION OF FAITH)

People of the mosque

THE POSITIONS OF PRAYER
The above pictures show a Muslim ritually washing himself and then praying. Muslims follow a fixed number of "bowings" while at prayer. There is a set sequence of movements, during which worshippers twice prostrate themselves (that is, kneel, then bow very low with their faces to the ground).

FOR MUSLIMS, ISLAM should rule over every part of the life of a person and of a nation, without any distinction between the religious and the rest. The mosque is central to the life of the community, and mosques may be centres for education and social work. The Qur'an lays down rules to govern, not just the life of an individual, but also the life of the community. These rules cover all areas of religious and social behaviour, from prayer, almsgiving, fasting, and pilgrimage, to marriage, inheritance, and food and drink. Also important are the Hadith (traditions), which record sayings and events in the life of Muhammad and the early Muslim communities. They contain the Sunnah (example) of the Prophet, the standard to which all Muslims should aspire. The Qur'an and Sunnah have combined to form the Shari'ah (law) which is a comprehensive guide to life and conduct giving a fixed code of behaviour for Muslims to follow.

CALL TO PRAYER
Five times a day, Muslims are called to prayer by a muezzin, who cries out from a minaret (a tower in a mosque, built for this purpose). Muezzins call in Arabic, beginning "God is most great" and ending "There is no god but God!"

AT THE MOSQUE
The mosque consists of an outer courtyard with running water where worshippers perform ritual washings to prepare themselves for prayer, and a large inner area. This is usually covered in carpets and rugs, and unfurnished except for pulpit, lectern, and platform. Here people pray, and also hear a sermon at the main weekly service on Friday afternoons.

This mosque, the Badshahi mosque in Lahore, Pakistan, one of the largest in the world, can hold nearly 100,000 worshippers

Worshippers approach the mosque quietly, leave their shoes at the entrance, and ritually wash themselves

SUFISM
A movement within Islam called Sufism focuses on the direct experience of God. Sufism is found within both branches of Islam, Sunni and Shi'ite. Some Sufis dance as part of their worship. The dancers are popularly known as "whirling dervishes".

Allahu akbar –
God is greater

CALL TO PRAYER FROM THE MINARET

PUBLIC PRAYERS
These worshippers, led by an imam (religious teacher), are prostrating themselves as they pray. As they bow they say "Glory be to my Lord, the great." As they prostrate themselves they say "Glory be to my Lord the almighty." The megaphone ensures that all worshippers can hear and follow the leader.

Compass shows the way to Mecca

PRAYER MAT
When Muslims pray, they face the Ka'bah in Mecca. To find the direction in which to pray, which is called the qiblah, they need a special compass. The compass is an integral part of many modern prayer mats like the one pictured here. Many Islamic countries such as Iran and Turkey have a tradition of weaving wonderful carpets and prayer rugs.

Shi'ite standard bearing the names of God, Muhammad, and Ali

SUNNI AND SHI'ITE
Sunni is the majority (90%) and Shi'ite the minority (10%) branch of Islam. Sunni Muslims see the Shari'ah, made by agreement of the community, as their vital guide, and believe that after Muhammad's death the caliphs (rulers) who succeeded him were his rightful successors. Shi'ite Muslims believe that only the descendants of Muhammad's daughter Fatima and her husband Ali should succeed him. They believe that after Ali died God sent Imams descended from Ali as His infallible messengers.

Index

Acknowledgments

Dorling Kindersley would like to thank:
The Ashmolean Museum (Andrew Topsfield); Surinder Singh Attariwala; The British Museum (Richard Blurton, Dylan Jackson, Graham Javes, Chris Kirby, Jane Newsom); The Buddhapadipa Temple (Venerable Phrakru Lom); The Central London Gurdwara (Bhupinder Bhasin Singh); David and Barbara Farbey; Glasgow Museums (Patricia Bascom, Jim Dunn, Ellen Howden, Antonia Lovelace, Mark O'Neil, Winnie Tyrell); Golders Green United Synagogue (Philip Solomons); Dr Ian L. Harris, Principal Lecturer in Religious Studies, University College of St Martin, Lancaster; Professor John Hinnells, Professor of Comparative Religion, School of Oriental and African Studies, University of London; Dora Holzhandler; The Jewish Museum, London (Alisa Jaffa); New World Aurora, Neal's Yard, Covent Garden; The Powell-Cotton Museum, Birchington, Kent (Derek and Sonja Howlett, Malcolm Harman); Dr John Shepherd, Reader in Religious Studies, University College of St Martin, Lancaster; Indarjit Singh; K. S. Singh; Westminster Cathedral (Father Mark Langham); The Zoroastrian Trust Funds of Europe (Incorporated) (Rusi Dalal)

Design, research, and editorial help:
Susila Baybars, Ann Cannings, Miriam Farbey, Julie Ferris, Jason Gonsalves, Iain Morris, Andrew Nash, Sailesh Patel, Kati Poynor, Miranda Smith, Helena Spiteri, Nicki Waine

Artwork: Sallie Alane Reason

Endpapers: Iain Morris

Index: Marion Dent

Additional photography: Janet Peckham at the British Museum

Picture credits
(a = above, b = below, c = centre, l = left, r = right, t = top)

The American Museum of Natural History, New York (Cat. No. 16/1507): 17bl;
Ancient Art & Architecture Collection: 55tr;
A.S.A.P. /Gadi Geffen: 46bl;
Ashmolean Museum, Oxford: 53tl;
Bridgeman Art Library, London /Victoria & Albert Museum, London: 21tl, /Bibliotheque Nationale, Paris: 30tl, /British Library: 36tl, 52br, /Giraudon/ Musée Condée, Chantilly: Front Cover c & 49, /Oriental Museum, Durham University: 25r, /Osma-Soria Chapter House, Soria/Index: 51bl, /Staatliche Museen, Berlin: 13tl, /Staats-und Universitatsbibliothek, Hamburg: 42tl, /Tretyakov Gallery, Moscow: 48c;
British Library: 52bl, Back Cover bl & 56l;
British Museum: 4c, 10-11b, 10tr, 10c, 10tl, 11tc, 11tl, 11cl, 12br, 12tl, 12bl, Front Cover bc & 57tl;
E.T. Archive /National Museum of Denmark: 53tr;
Mary Evans Picture Library: 20tr, 31bcl, 58tr;
Werner Forman Archive: 8tr, 34tr;
Photographie Giraudon /Musée Condée, Chantilly: 57br, /Musée Guimet, Paris: 24br;
Glasgow Museums: The Burrell Collection: 13l, 31br, Back Cover tl & 51br, /St Mungo Museum of Religious Life & Art: 15r, © Dora Holzhandler 46br;
Sally & Richard Greenhill /Sam Greenhill: 28tl;
Sonia Halliday Photographs: 12tr, 42c;
Robert Harding Picture Library: 8tl, 9tl, 16tr, 22tl, 22bl, 26cr, 26tl, 34tl, 38rc, 44tr, 52tr, 54c, 59c;
Hutchison Library: 14c, /Nick Haslam: 29bl, /Emile Salmanov: 41tr, /Michael MacIntyre: 35tr;
Images Colour Library: 32bl;
Impact /Christopher Cormack: 38lc, /G. Mermet/Cedri: 25tr, /Mohamed Ansar: 22tr;
Joods Historisch Museum, Amsterdam: 44tl;
Magnum /Abbas: 56tr, /Bruno Barbey: 8br, 40rc, 40lc, /Fred Mayer: 33br;
Nelson-Atkins Museum of Art, Kansas City, Missouri (Gift of Bronson Trevor in honor of his father, John Trevor): 30tr;
Panos Pictures /Paul Smith: 52cl;
Ann & Bury Peerless: 37bl, Front Cover lac & 39tl, 58-59b;
Pitt Rivers Museum, Oxford: 32-33b;
Peter Sanders: 54-55b, 54bl, 58tl;
Scala, Florence /Bargello, Florence: 48tr, /Museo di S. Marco, Florence: 50b, 53br, / St Peter's, The Vatican, Rome: 50tr;
Spectrum Colour Library: 34bl;
Frank Spooner Pictures: 20tl, /Bartholome/Liaison: 37tl;
Museum of the Order of St John: 50tl;
Tony Stone Images /Patrick Ward: 8-9c;
Topham Picture Source: 30bl;
Trip /H. Rogers: 38tl;
ZEFA Pictures: 45cl

EYEWITNESS GUIDES

SUBJECTS

HISTORY

AFRICA

ARMS & ARMOUR

BATTLE

CASTLE

CHINA

COWBOY

EXPLORER

KNIGHT

MEDIEVAL LIFE

MYTHOLOGY

NORTH AMERICAN INDIAN

PIRATE

PRESIDENTS

RUSSIA

SHIPWRECK

TITANIC

VIKING

WITCH & WIZARD

ANCIENT WORLDS

ANCIENT EGYPT

ANCIENT GREECE

ANCIENT ROME

AZTEC

BIBLE LANDS

MUMMY

PYRAMID

THE BEGINNINGS OF LIFE

ARCHAEOLOGY

DINOSAUR

EARLY PEOPLE

PREHISTORIC LIFE

THE ARTS

CINEMA

COSTUME

DANCE

MUSIC

WRITING

TECHNOLOGY

BOAT

CAR

FLYING MACHINE

FUTURE

INVENTION

SPACE EXPLORATION

TRAIN

PAINTING

GOYA

IMPRESSIONISM

LEONARDO

MANET

MONET

PERSPECTIVE

RENAISSANCE

VAN GOGH

WATERCOLOUR

SCIENCE

ASTRONOMY

CHEMISTRY

EARTH

ECOLOGY

ELECTRICITY

ELECTRONICS

ENERGY

EVOLUTION

FORCE & MOTION

HUMAN BODY

LIFE

LIGHT

MATTER

MEDICINE

SKELETON

TECHNOLOGY

TIME & SPACE

SPORT

AMERICAN FOOTBALL

BASEBALL

FOOTBALL

OLYMPICS

SPORT

ANIMALS

AMPHIBIAN

BIRD

BUTTERFLY & MOTH

CAT

DOG

EAGLE

ELEPHANT

FISH

GORILLA

HORSE

INSECT

MAMMAL

REPTILE

SHARK

WHALE

HABITATS

ARCTIC & ANTARCTIC

DESERT

JUNGLE

OCEAN

POND & RIVER

SEASHORE

THE EARTH

CRYSTAL & GEM

FOSSIL

HURRICANE & TORNADO

PLANT

ROCK & MINERAL

SHELL

TREE

VOLCANO

WEATHER

THE WORLD AROUND US

BUILDING

CRIME & DETECTION

FARM

FLAG

MEDIA

MONEY

RELIGION

SPY

Future updates and editions will be available online at www.dk.com

A–Z

DK EYEWITNESS GUIDES

1–110

Future updates and editions will be available online at www.dk.com

Stock-take 2013